FAST TRAIN RUSSIA

FAST
TRAIN
RUSSIA

Jay Higginbotham

Dodd, Mead & Company † New York

Library of Congress Cataloging in Publication Data

Higginbotham, Jay.
  Fast train Russia.

  1. Soviet Union—Description and travel—
1945-   . 2. Higginbotham, Jay. I. Title.
DK28.H48   1983   914.7'04853   82-23514
ISBN 0-396-08156-8

1   2   3   4   5   6   7   8   9   10

For my wife, Louisa,
and my children, Jeanne, Denis, and Robert

"There is a saying in the Orient: 'What is stronger than stone? What is more powerful than fire?' And the answer is—the friendship of peoples."

—*Mikhail Georgadze*

PROLOGUE

Fiery crosses, civil rights marches, antiwar crusades, student revolt—such were the hallmarks of America in the 1960s, during which decade I passed my early manhood. Deep, dark divisions, beyond which loomed the ever-present Cold War, shook the nation's confidence and stability.

In the midst of this fume and ferment—in the summer of 1966—I set out from my home in Mobile, Alabama, on a vagabond journey around the world. I was single, carefree, a quixotic twenty-eight—but with a certain earnest curiosity to see what the planet was like beyond the spectra of race riots and assassinations and alienated youth.

The seething sixties had long passed, however, and my trip was a receded memory when, one late-winter day, a tall, square-shouldered man stopped by my desk at the Mobile Public Library, where I was employed as head of the Local History section, and asked if we had any books by Russian authors.

"Russian authors . . . ?" I repeated, vacantly. I'd been deeply engrossed in drawing up a monthly report, but the question struck me as slightly odd. "Of course," I said, finally. "We have lots of books by Russian authors. Why do you ask?"

"But the girl at the desk said you had no such books," insisted the man, and at that point I noticed a faint, barely familiar accent.

"No, that's not correct," I answered. "She must have misunderstood you. We have quite a few works by Russian authors—Turgenev, Chekhov . . . probably everything written by Tolstoy and Dostoevsky." I got up from my desk and said, "Come on, I'll help you find them."

"No, it's not necessary," the man replied. "I was only curious." Then he introduced himself. He was, he said, Lev Knjazev, an author from the Far Eastern city of Vladivostok. He was a passenger on the *Anton Chekhov*, a large freighter docked at the port of Mobile, and was gathering material for a series of travel articles he was doing for a Moscow newspaper.

"Oh, you're from the Soviet Union," I said, extending my hand. "I was in the USSR myself once, years ago— back when I was teaching school and had my summers free." When his face brightened I went on to describe how in the summer of 1966, purely on some youthful whim, I'd struck out on a trip around the world, the most memorable segment of which took me across Russia from the Sea of Japan to the beaches of Odessa.

This information sparked a warm but unavoidably

brief conversation, at the end of which, on some offhand impulse, I invited Lev to my home that evening. "I'd like my wife and children to meet you," I explained.

"You would?" he asked. He seemed taken aback, as though he hadn't quite heard me correctly. I repeated the invitation and when finally he accepted I made arrangements to pick him up at the *Anton Chekhov* at seven o'clock.

That night, Lev and I and several companions he brought along from the ship spent a convivial evening together comparing impressions of our respective countries. We sipped drinks and swapped travel stories far into the night and I couldn't resist elaborating on my Russian experiences. For me it was like a reunion of sorts, since these were the first Russians I'd come into contact with since I returned from the Soviet Union nearly thirteen years before.

Over the weekend my family and I saw a bit more of Lev Knjazev and his friends. Two days following their visit to our home, we spent a pleasant Sunday afternoon aboard the *Anton Chekhov.* My children—Jeanne, Denis, and Robert—were ecstatic at being able to tour a Soviet ship, and my wife, Louisa, and I brought some small gifts for Lev and his comrades, only to find that they had several for us also.

Later that afternoon we had a quiet meal in Lev's spacious cabin, and our conversation turned once more to my Russian encounters, to people I had met while crossing Siberia—at the height of the war in Vietnam, when not-far-distant American bombers were pounding Hanoi. Just before we left that evening, Lev suggested I ought to write about those times, about my travels through his country—something on the "personal" side. "From what you've told me," he said, "I think such an account would prove quite intriguing—not only to Americans but to Russians as well."

I doubted that my travel experiences, as compelling as they were to me personally, would be of much interest to anyone outside a close circle of family and friends. Nevertheless, in the weeks following the departure of the *Anton Chekhov*, I found I couldn't so easily put Lev's suggestion aside. Wherever I turned, the memories of certain people and places and incidents—especially those gained while crossing the vast continent of Asia by rail—kept flooding my waking hours.

Fortunately, I had kept a journal—a small, canvas-covered book I'd picked up in Japan just before I left Yokohama for the Asia coast. All the way through Russia and around the world, I kept this journal in my hip pocket and was diligent in making my daily entries. On returning to America, I stored the journal in a rolltop desk in my bachelor's apartment, lending it on occasion to friends and relatives. Finally I lost track of it during the course of moving several times—the last time into a large two-story house following my marriage and the birth of my children. I had never taken time to read back over it, although I always planned to someday.

Eventually I retrieved the old journal, with its worn and closely written pages, from a box of papers in the attic. Poring over the spidery entries, I began the task of re-creating the events of my Russian adventure, all the while maintaining a lively correspondence with Lev Knjazev, who was full of plans for "our" project.

When I finished the story I sent the manuscript on to Vladivostok and waited for Lev's reaction. He never received the package, however, and after five or six more attempts—all mysteriously abortive—I hit on the idea of sending the manuscript one page at a time in my letters. Lev's response, as he digested the "serialization," was warmly enthusiastic, and he proceeded to translate it into Russian while working out details for printing it in a literary journal.

Since that time, events seem to have taken on a life of their own: the publication of the book in Russia; its exhibition at the International Book Fair in Moscow; the movement in Mobile to establish a sister-city relationship with a Soviet city; an invitation for my family to visit Russia; Lev's plans for his family to visit mine; and now the publication of the book in English.

No glimmering of such possibilities entered my head, however, on that cool afternoon in my attic. As I sat there in the faint light, rereading entries first made in the summer of 1966, a host of visions entombed in the past began once more to stir in my memory. Voices and faces lost in the dust of years began to speak and move again—amid the whir and roar of churning locomotives on the plains of Siberia—above the slapping of waves on the Sea of Japan . . .

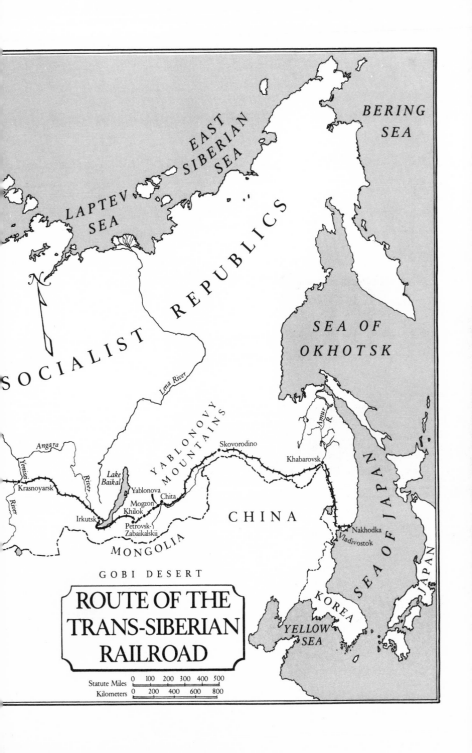

BERING
SEA

EAST
SIBERIAN
SEA

LAPTEV
SEA

REPUBLICS

SOCIALIST

SEA OF
OKHOTSK

Lena River

YABLONOVY
MOUNTAINS

Angara

Amur R.

Skovorodino

Khabarovsk

Yenisei

Lake
Baikal

River

Krasnoyarsk

Yablonova

Chita

SEA OF JAPAN

Mogzon

CHINA

Khilok

River

Irkutsk

Nakhodka

Petrovsk-
Zabaikalskii

Vladivostok

MONGOLIA

JAPAN

GOBI DESERT

KOREA

ROUTE OF THE
TRANS-SIBERIAN
RAILROAD

YELLOW
SEA

Statute Miles   0   100   200   300   400   500
Kilometers   0   200   400   600   800

FAST TRAIN RUSSIA

JULY 7, 1966—*We are moving northward on the Pacific Ocean, on the Russian steamer M/S* Baikal, *a gleaming white vessel that doesn't seem to be taking the seas so well. I always pictured the Pacific as being rather calm and serene, but it's a little rougher than I expected. Already I am beginning to feel woozy and we have been gone from Yokohama less than six hours. Outside my window hazy sunlight is glistening on the water's surface and every now and then I see a jumping fish through a faint wisp of shifting fog. . . .*

This was my first voyage on the sea in more than two years, and I'd forgotten that it took some getting used to. I had just spent three very pleasant weeks in Japan, where I stayed with some American friends at the U.S. Air Force Base at Tachikawa, just outside of Tokyo. Frequently, during those three weeks, I had contemplated the next leg of my around-the-world journey: the section that had been arranged by Intourist to take me through the heart of Russia on the Trans-Siberian railway, from Nakhodka to Moscow. The idea of making this excursion had filled me with expectation; it was, after all, the longest train ride in the world—nearly six thousand miles from beginning to end—over some of the most remarkable terrain on earth. Yet the thought of such a trip also sharpened my anxiety. I knew very little about Russia, about the people and their customs, and not more than two words of the language. How would I fare in such an unfamiliar land? Chances were, I wouldn't be treated in a very hospitable manner. This possibility occurred to me quite often as I daily watched American supply planes taking off from Tachikawa, bound for Vietnam. And perhaps worse, what kind of accommodations would there be on the Trans-Siberian railway? Was it possible I might be standing up the entire trip (as I would later be forced to do on a harrowing midnight journey from Cairo to Luxor)? Would I soon regret taking this northern route to Europe, rather than a southern course through Hong Kong, India, and Iran? Even the region's name filled me with a certain awe: Siberia!—a prodigious, unthawed wilderness; a savage wasteland where exiles grubbed their lives away in worthless mines and carnivorous beasts stalked human beings across vast, unmarked reaches of frozen tundra.

With such misgivings still in mind, I passed the first afternoon on the M/S *Baikal*. By four o'clock my wooziness had increased, so I went to my cabin and fell asleep, the waves slapping steadily against the *Baikal*'s hull.

Two hours later I arose, feeling a little steadier, although the ship was still swaying. After a short walk on deck I felt much better. My appetite was growing, so I went on to the dining room and was assigned a table. This, I anticipated, would be the trip's first high point. It would be good to meet some fellow passengers, to engage them in lively conversation.

At my table was a white-haired Australian government official, a young Russian engineer, and a middle-aged Japanese businessman. The Japanese seemed nervous, uttering hardly a word as we ate, and the Russian mumbled something only once, concentrating solely on his meal. But the Australian was a very big talker.

"Oh," he said, slyly. "So you're going on the Trans-Sib? Oho!" He laughed and winked at the other two. "Well, you'd better be careful, my friend. They'll put you in with your opposites for sure." He laughed again. "I *know*. I rode that train once myself—from Moscow to the Pacific. But," he added, "you'll get over it, eventually, I'm certain."

His mischievousness seemed foreboding. I was about to

ask him exactly what he meant by "opposites," when he went into a tirade about the war in Vietnam: "Not that I'm opposed to what you're doing there; but you're going about it all wrong, you know. What you *should* do is blow everything up all at once and quit this dallying around. But no, you bomb and retreat, bomb and retreat. What you're doing, you see, is creating a genuine mess that's eventually going to threaten the security of Australia as well as the stability of all Southeast Asia." I glanced at the Russian, but he seemed engrossed in his meal. "Oh, don't worry about him," the Australian said, "he doesn't understand any English." Then he launched into a blistering assault on both the communist manner of doing business and the greed of American capitalists.

After dinner, a little chagrined by the Aussie's rantings, I went back to my cabin and lay down for a while, reminiscing about our colorful send-off from the port of Yokohama and how different my mood had been then: the morning had been bright and sunny and there was a tingling excitement in the air, with thousands of confetti streamers strewn from the wharves to the decks of the ship. A large crowd had gathered on the pier, among them my friends from Tachikawa. As the *Baikal* pulled slowly away from the dock, severing the last confetti strands, and chugged through the inner harbor, a spirited band played a bouncy, rollicking tune. The crowd cheered and waved little flags and pennants. Standing on the *Baikal*'s deck and bidding my friends good-bye, I had felt a twinge of elation, an exhilaration at the reality of leaving for the great unknown land of Russia.

Now, however, the Yokohama send-off seemed far away and long ago. Confronted by a growing monotony and a roughening sea, my thoughts turned inward—toward the creaking, swaying ship and my own queasy stomach.

I awoke to a setting sun and strolled around deck, watching lonely lights from Japanese fishing boats blinking on the western horizon. The fresh, salty air seemed good for my queasiness. Just after dusk, I left the main deck and went down to the ship's library to finish the novel I had started that morning, but my stomach soon advised me of my mistake.

Up in the lounge, I found the Japanese businessman at the bar drinking alone. "Cognac good drink," he said, raising his glass and smiling. He seemed more affable than he had at supper, and I gathered that the cognac must be good indeed.

"Well," I said, sitting down next to him, "I'll have to see for myself."

With several more drinks under his belt, the Japanese became almost as talkative as the Aussie, but lost very little of his nervousness. Moreover, I quickly noticed something else about him: he stuttered badly. He had been, he said, a kamikaze pilot during the war. In fact, he'd been a squadron leader and had met personally with the famed Tojo on numerous occasions. He related in detail these meetings with his former leader, whom he now viewed as wicked and incompetent. (Somehow I had the feeling that his judgment of Tojo was purely for my benefit.) A few cognacs later, he described with great fervor how, near the end of the war, he was scheduled to lead an attack on an American fleet near Okinawa, but how on that occasion he never got off the ground. He was reported dead by the newspapers and returned "like a ghost" to his incredulous family and friends. After the war ended, he claimed, he was tried and almost condemned to death with Tojo and others.

It was difficult to tell how much of the fellow's story to believe. Perhaps all of it was true; perhaps he had only scratched the surface of his experiences. If so, it would no doubt explain the cause of his tremor and stammer. He was perfectly willing to describe in detail his own harrowing personal experiences—eager, in fact—but when I mentioned Hiroshima and Nagasaki, he fell strangely silent, his sharp black eyes settling into a dull stare. I watched him a moment, sorry I had brought up the subject. "No," he said, after a long pause, "but there were other bombings, almost as terrible. In Tokyo . . ." He stopped, his eyes beginning to redden. "I had a niece . . . ," he started to say, but he finally gave up, unable to continue.

I swallowed, took another sip of cognac, and after some moments, continued the conversation on another subject. It was only later, while drifting off to sleep in the darkness of my cabin, with the roar of waves in my ear, that my thoughts, and then my dreams, returned to that conversation—and to visions of fire bombs screaming in the night.

JULY 8—*It is now nearly noon. I woke up too late to eat breakfast this morning, but it's just as well. Eating is the farthest thing from my mind. I thought this ship was swaying a little yesterday. It wasn't. Compared to today, it was merely drifting along on fluffy white clouds. Now it's rocking and pitching and weaving, almost as if in distress. All I can see through the porthole are ponderous dark squall clouds above raging whitecaps, and over the roll of sloshing waves I hear the tapping of rain on the deck. Enough of this. I'm going back to the bunk.*

I finally got up a little after noon. After a half-hearted attempt at shaving, I made my way to the dining room, but there was hardly anyone present and all I ate was some dark dry bread and a bowl of lumpy soup that the stewardess called *solyanka*. Apparently none of my table-mates had even shown up.

Out on deck, the rain had stopped momentarily, but a heavy mist still hung in the air. I saw the Japanese leaning over the rail, looking wistfully out to sea. I started to go over, then turned back abruptly. The conversation in the bar the night before had depressed me deeply and I didn't feel like starting another one. Instead, I walked down the side deck and stepped into the ship's library, where I found the Australian flipping through a magazine.

"You don't look so well," he said, looking up and grinning.

"I don't feel so well," I replied.

"Well, you'll get used to it," he laughed. "Trouble is, by the time you get used to it, we'll be out of it." He laughed again, as if the thought of someone else's discomfiture gave him considerable pleasure. "Nonetheless," he added, "we'll be on past the straits by morning and things will be better on the Sea of Japan. You know about the straits?"

I said that I didn't, and that at the moment I didn't particularly care, but nothing would stop him from telling me.

"The Tsugaru Straits are actually very treacherous," he said. "I *know*; I've been through them a hundred times.

It's much worse in winter, though, so count your blessings. However, I can see already it's going to be a rough night. In fact, the Pacific here is about the worst I've ever seen it at this time of year. How're you feeling *now?*"

I said I still felt terrible.

"I thought Americans were supposed to be tough," he said.

"You've been seeing too many John Wayne movies," I muttered, but he didn't seem to notice my remark. By this time he was off on another facet of my future: "But you're in for an even rougher time, you know, if you're going on that trip to Moscow. I don't envy you, that's for sure. No, I don't envy you a-tall. I've been on that ride myself, you know."

"Yes, you mentioned it," I said.

"And I'll tell you, I'd much rather be on a ship, under any conditions, than on a train. On a ship you can always walk out on deck for a breath of fresh air—but on a train . . . well, it's so . . . suffocating. And so bloody monotonous. No, I don't envy you a-tall, my friend. Not a-tall."

"I think I'll get some of that fresh air you were talking about," I said, and excused myself.

"Oh, it'll get better," he said, as I was leaving. "Just wait till we get to the Sea of Japan."

But the Sea of Japan seemed a long way off. Later that afternoon, when we entered the dreaded straits (between Honshu and Hokkaido), the ship began rocking worse than ever. Despite the weather, I stood on deck, watching the sun disappear through heavy black clouds, watching

stray birds and lonely lighthouses and corroded old trawl-
ers lurching in the sea. Then I was driven indoors by
resurgent rains and cool, whipping winds.

Inside the lounge, doors were banging, glasses and
plates were rolling off tables, and the creaking and groan-
ing of the woodwork sounded as if the *Baikal* were ready
to split apart. Riotous waves were pounding the ship's
hull, seeming to explode on impact, and the surge and
plunge of the bow and stern gave a feeling of absurd
buoyancy, as though we were in a rapidly descending
elevator.

A few minutes after I entered, I left the lounge and
hastened to my cabin where, green with nausea, I threw
up in the sink—then fell across my bunk and slept like a
slowly revolving log for over three hours.

Just after nine o'clock I got up and headed back to the
lounge again. The ship was still tossing, but more evenly,
and there didn't seem to be as strong a crosscurrent.

The lounge was deserted. The whole ship, in fact,
seemed deserted. I stepped out on deck, listening to the
roaring wind and the sloshing of tumultuous waves, then
staggered back inside where this time I found the barmaid
and the Japanese businessman. The Japanese didn't seem
as glad to see me as he had the previous night, but raised
his glass anyway and slurred, "More c-cognac for you?"
A short while later he left, and two more Japanese came
in—one a teacher of French named Gatsuo, the other an
artist called Gashi. They said they were both going to

Paris via the Trans-Siberian railway. This struck me as excellent news. We had a long and cheery conversation —the most promising I'd yet had with anyone—and for a while I felt relieved, believing I had found agreeable company for the long trip to Moscow.

After drinks, however, the Japanese invited me to their cabin, where Gashi showed me photographs of his paintings—most of which were utterly startling. The paintings were all either morose or tragic or incredibly hideous: there were ramshackle houses, blighted landscapes, disfigured women, deformed infants, etc. When I asked him why he painted such grotesque pictures, he remarked, with a lewd smile, "Because beauty is not a fit subject for art."

I thought Gashi's view of aesthetics rather incongruous, considering his sunny disposition, and that night I had more bad dreams, this time of misshapen trees, of limbless sumo wrestlers, and children with holes in their heads.

JULY 9—*God, what a night we had. Contrary to what the Aussie told me, the Sea of Japan is extremely turbulent, perhaps, however, beginning to calm a bit as we get farther away from the straits. But the rain has started up again and the fog has become very dense. My nausea seems to have passed; for good, I hope. This morning only the Russian and I made it for breakfast. The Aussie is possibly not as tough as he thought, but no doubt he'll have another explanation for his absence. . . .*

After breakfast I spent most of the morning in the library reading magazines and writing in my journal, then went outside and walked around on deck for a while. The rain was finally beginning to let up a little. We were, I guessed, still several hundred miles off the coast of Asia, but I had no certain knowledge as to exactly where, or even in which direction, we were headed. Looking out from the ship, I could see nothing but fog and low-flying gray clouds on every side. We seemed to be in the middle of nowhere, heading nowhere at approximately seventeen knots. I played Ping-Pong with a Filipino boy and watched some documentary films in the music salon (travelogues of Turkestan and Karelia: all in Russian, but very exotic and seductive). I then made my way to the dining room where my three tablemates had already begun eating.

The meal was half finished when the Aussie commenced his travel lecture. "The Bay of Nakhodka," he announced, "which we shall be approaching later this afternoon, was not discovered until 1859—by sailors from a Russian ship called *America.*" He paused, waiting for my reaction, and when I showed none he continued: "The name of the ship was not so strange as it might seem, however, because you see at that time Russia still owned Alaska and still, in fact, had certain possessions in California. Does that surprise you?"

"No," I said, "nothing surprises me."

"No?" he said. "Well, it surprises most people. I suppose you must have some knowledge of history—which is extraordinary for an American, to say the least. In any case, a terrific storm arose one night and the *America* sank and the sailors drifted along on makeshift lifeboats for days and days without hope of ever seeing land again. But then one morning a benign current carried them safely into an inlet—into a bay of such breathtaking beauty that they called it 'Nakhodka.' "

He paused again to allow me the opportunity to ask the obvious question, and this time I didn't disappoint him.

"It means," he said, " 'godsend, the unexpectedly found.' " He looked triumphantly at me, then at the Japanese, then finally at the Russian. The Japanese smiled thinly, as if he knew the story already, but the Russian only stared at his soup bowl.

"That's very interesting," I finally said.

"Yes, it is," he replied, "but we shall very soon see whether or not it's so breathtaking in its beauty as legend has made it. And I think the answer to that *will* surprise you." He then settled into an extended description of Nakhodka's more recent history, by the end of which the Japanese and I had both joined the Russian in staring at our soup bowls.

After lunch, I retired to my cabin to pack my suitcase and take a short nap. When I emerged around two o'clock the sun had broken through the clouds, the fog had completely lifted, and in the distance we could see the barren coast of Asia. "Nakhodka!" one of the crewmen yelled at me, pointing farther west, but I couldn't see very much.

I stood there watching what looked like mud lumps edging slowly toward us, then went back to the dining room for tea.

"The Japanese is chomping at the bit to get off ship," the Aussie said, when I walked in. "So he won't be with us this afternoon."

I nodded, glancing at the other empty chair. "And the Russian?"

"Who knows about the Russian," he said, shrugging.

We sat there, drinking tea and nibbling on some large brown cookies. "Well," said the Aussie, "in an hour or so we'll be leaving ship and you'll be boarding your train for Moscow. I must say once again, I don't envy you a bit. You've got quite a long ride ahead of you, you know. Did you bring some reading material?"

"Not much," I answered.

"No?" he said, shaking his head. "It's just as well then. The train rocks and rolls so much you wouldn't be able to read, anyway. The thing that's going to get you, though, is the incredible boredom you'll have to put up with. There's absolutely nothing to do, you see, but just sit there and watch these wretched little villages appear and disappear along the tracks. Sometimes I think monotony is man's most formidable foe. And the Russians won't be too friendly toward you, either. They're mighty incensed at Americans these days. Did you notice how this chap sitting with us behaved? Did you notice how he just sat there, as though none of us even existed?"

"But he doesn't speak any English," I said.

"All the same, that's pretty much the way they are. You'll encounter that all along the way, I assure you. Don't tell me, I know 'em. They're the coldest sort of folk —colder than frozen fish. Why, I don't know. Maybe it's the weather. Whatever the reason, they have these unbending beliefs, these . . . regulations—and they don't budge an inch. Not for anything. Tell me, why didn't you fly?"

I was thinking that maybe I should have; but by that time the Aussie was pointing toward the window, saying, "Aha! We approach the great port of Nakhodka. Do you see there?"

I got up from the table and went to the window, peering out at a relatively spacious harbor filled with many ships, large and small. Beyond the harbor an arc of green-brown hills rose sharply in the near background, with lonely white cottages dotting the hillsides. At the foot of the hills was the town itself, which seemed unusually desolate—devoid of both people and movement. In a word, it looked dead.

When I returned to the table the Aussie asked, "Now that you've had a glimpse of her, does Nakhodka strike you as a godsend?"

"Looks pretty bleak," I admitted.

"A mere portent, my friend. A mere portent of things to come."

That was the last I saw of the Aussie. An hour later, I left the *Baikal* and was hustled through a stucco customs station where I exchanged a hundred American dollars for rubles and kopeks and was ordered to unload my suitcase.

"We must not allow these," a uniformed official announced, punching at two *Time* magazines, but handing me back a paperback novel.

I started to ask why, then quickly thought better of it. Instead, I stuffed the rubles in my wallet and was hurried to a large platform where two green coaches were being hitched to eight other coaches. I stood there a good ten minutes, entranced by the operation, trying to get used to the fact that I was actually on Soviet soil. The sun had disappeared behind the nearby hills and a soft pink twilight had set in, clothing the sky in a mystical haze that seemed to hang interminably above the town and station. Looking around, I noticed that everything appeared to have quit moving; there was an uneasy, almost eerie silence, as though the human race had ceased to exist. "Where has everyone gone?" I wondered. I began walking down the platform, toward the locomotive, trying to find a place to get on the train, when a voice suddenly rang out behind me: "You will come with me, please!"

Turning, I followed a black-coated woman on up the platform, eventually being ushered onto a rear coach and then into a quaint but plush-looking compartment. "You will stay here," the woman said sternly, glancing around.

"Yes, thanks," I said, "can you tell me where—"

"Yes," she said. "You will stay here." She pointed to

the top bunk on the side toward the middle of the coach, then abruptly disappeared.

I tossed my suitcase on the top bunk, looking the compartment over more carefully. The bunks seemed soft enough, and there was a small table jutting out from the window with a trash container hooked underneath. On the floor was a thick, turquoise rug with exotic, oriental-looking designs. Behind the table were some cream-colored curtains. I sat down on the lower bunk a moment, waiting for something to happen, and when nothing did, I stepped outside the compartment, fully expecting the woman to come back and say, "You will stay here, please." But she didn't. In fact, I saw no one, so I continued on down the corridor, brushing against the wine-colored curtains and walking silently over the carpeted floor. Once, I stopped and pulled back the curtains, peering out at the platform, but still no one was in sight. "Where the devil *is* everybody?" I wondered. I moved farther down the corridor, observing the gleaming mirrors, the polished brass fittings, and the roman numerals on the compartment doors. Then I crossed into another car, almost bumping into a heavily wrinkled woman aggressively sweeping the passageway with a brushwood broom. She raised up when I approached, grunted something unintelligible, then went back to her work.

Eventually I made my way to the dining car, which was filled with people—all noisily eating. "So this is where everybody is," I thought. I sat down at one of the tables, relieved to be back among the human race. Sometime later I was brought a menu, the script on which appeared to be mirror writing. I pointed to a couple of items and shortly was served an egg roll and a bowl of soup, which the stewardess called *borscht*. None of it looked very appetizing, but I downed it all anyway. Then I lit a cigarette and began sipping at a glass of sherry, searching the diner for any familiar faces that might have been with me on the *Baikal*. The only people I really expected to see were the two Japanese—the artist Gashi and the teacher Gatsuo, who I knew were also going to Moscow; but neither was anywhere to be seen.

Then suddenly the train jerked, and slowly we began to move forward. "Well," I sighed. "We're off at last." I looked out the window at the creeping landscape, now almost hidden by the rapidly falling darkness, and settled back in my seat.

For a long time, as the engine gradually picked up speed, I sat staring out the window, smoking and drinking and watching occasional lights flicker past the glass, until the flickering became less and less frequent, finally disappearing completely in the blackness of night. From my map I knew that the route to Khabarovsk—the first large city on our itinerary—hugged the eastern boundary of China, and I was disappointed that I wasn't able to see any of the countryside. "Well, maybe in the morning," I thought. I had no idea at that point when we would be reaching Khabarovsk.

For nearly an hour I remained in the dining car, hoping

to meet someone I could talk to. There was no use going back to my compartment, with absolutely nothing to do. In time, however, the dining car cleared out. I was the only one left and the stewardesses kept glaring in my direction, obviously anxious for me to leave.

Finally, I got up and walked back through the rear door of the diner, then on to the next car, passing in the corridor a number of passengers clad in bright striped pajamas. When I arrived back at my compartment I opened the sliding door and stopped—and then I knew what the Aussie meant when he said, "They'll put you in with your opposites." For sitting on the lower bed across from my bunk was a woman—with a young boy beside her—and above them, on the upper bunk, a heavyset blond-haired man. They looked as surprised to see me as I was to see them.

After a moment, I said, "Good evening," but they only stared back and looked uncertainly at one another.

"*No specken Deutsch,*" the man finally said, with the barest trace of a smile. His wife looked at me, gaping—as did the small boy, who appeared to be about age six or seven.

I nodded, trying to smile back, then extended my hand and said, "Me . . . *Amerikansky.*" I wasn't even sure this was a genuine Russian word, but the man bobbed his head, as though he understood, before limply taking my hand. "*Amerikansky,*" he repeated, with little hint of enthusiasm, then spoke at length to his wife and child. The only word I could make out was "*Amerikanets.*" He then pointed to himself and said, "Vova," and to his son, say-ing, "Yuri." I didn't quite catch his wife's name. I touched my chest and said, "Jay," and he nodded and said, "Zhay . . . Zhay" several times. After that, there didn't seem to be much else to say. I pointed to my bunk a few times to indicate where I was sleeping. Vova looked at me and nodded. The mother and Yuri only gazed back impas-sively.

By this time it was around nine o'clock and I was puzzled about what to do next. I hadn't been to bed this early in twenty years, but I couldn't stand in the corridor all night. There was no lounge, the dining room was closed—there was simply nothing to do. Deciding to turn in, I looked back at the three Russians, who were still staring. They were all in their pajamas. Then it struck me: How was I going to get undressed? Besides this tactical problem, I had nothing to change *into*. It never occurred to me to bring along my pajamas.

"Excuse me," I said, backing out the door. "I'm going for a smoke." I strode down the corridor, wondering how in hell this arrangement was going to work. Obviously, things couldn't go on like this all the way to Moscow. Or could they? I felt like kicking myself for not having packed a pair of pajamas—and a Russian phrasebook; two very useful items, I concluded. I lit a cigarette and stood there peering out the window into the darkness.

It finally hit me that there was only one thing to do: I would sleep in my clothes, at least for the night. I stubbed out my cigarette, stumbled back to the compartment, waved to my stolid bunkmates, and retrieved my tooth-brush and paste. I then headed for the washroom, where I found that brushing my teeth was not so easy a chore: the train was creaking and swaying very badly and it was all I could do to remain upright.

When I returned to the compartment the second time, the lights were out. I put my toothbrush back in my shaving kit, climbed onto the top bunk, pulled the blanket over me, and tried valiantly to drop off to sleep. But sleep was long in coming. Over and over, as the train rumbled on through the night, I could hear the Aussie's warnings drifting back to me: "I don't envy you a bit, my friend. No, not a bit. Tell me, why didn't you fly?"

JULY 10—*We must be about a hundred miles from Khabarovsk. Or so it would seem by the map. I am sitting in the dining car, gazing out the window at the distant hills of Manchurian China, having just finished a breakfast of toast, jelly, an omelette, and tea. For endless miles in front of the hills a savage underbrush, thick and junglelike, pervades the countryside, and somewhere in the midst of it I envision the fabled ginseng weed and the Siberian tiger. . . .*

I wondered why it was called the Siberian tiger; technically, we were still in the section known to the Soviets as the Far East and would not enter Siberia for at least two more days. Maybe the beast was native to Siberia and had only migrated to Manchuria in recent centuries. If so, it couldn't have chosen a more impregnable habitat. The entire morning, through the heart of a rugged, almost unscarred wilderness, I saw not a single paved highway. No wonder the Russians attached so much importance to this railroad, I mused. It was their only real link to the Far East and the ports of Nakhodka and Vladivostok. Nonetheless, the security here appeared rather tenuous, the line hugging the Chinese border as closely as it did. Observing the paucity of people and settlements along the tracks, it seemed likely to me that Peking could sever this East-West link with very little effort if it had to, or really wanted to. Not without inviting quick retaliation, I supposed, but the situation seemed plausible. If World War III ever erupted, this might well be where it would begin.

The train was moving at a rather slow pace—perhaps thirty miles per hour—and not too smoothly. As far as I knew, we had been traveling continuously for at least thirteen hours. If we had stopped during the night, we had not stopped for long. In truth, there seemed little reason to. By ten o'clock we were still chugging through a primitive, almost uninhabited hinterland. Only occasionally did I see a log cabin, a small patch of farmland, or a horse-drawn wagon.

My cabinmates had still been asleep when I left for breakfast, but when I got back to the compartment they were up and about, still in their pajamas. Vova had just returned from the washroom. He was grimacing and rubbing his face with a lotion, which reminded me that I should be doing something I dreaded, something I had never done before: shave on a moving train. Maybe I should wait until we reach Khabarovsk, I thought. No, maybe there wouldn't be time. I had no idea what our schedule would be when we got to Khabarovsk. Better to get it over with now. On the other hand, maybe there would be a stop *before* we reached Khabarovsk.

Still debating the idea, I decided to do something else instead. I opened my suitcase and got out my camera. I had pulled back the curtain and was about to snap a picture of the countryside when I felt a tapping on my shoulder. Turning around quickly, I saw Vova standing behind me, shaking his head gravely. Among the unfamiliar sounds he was making I thought I heard the word *nyet*. He was pointing toward the door, still shaking his head. I looked at Vova's wife and son staring grimly back at me, hesitated a moment, then slowly put my camera away. "*Nyet?*" I asked him.

"*Nyet*," he said, seemingly satisfied.

I then decided it was a good time to shave after all, so I picked up my kit and hurried off to the washroom.

It wasn't so bad as I'd imagined, but it wasn't so comfortable, either. Not only was I swaying from side to side, knocking my elbows alternately against the window and light switch, but to my great dismay I discovered there was no hot water. I did manage to finish the task without slitting my throat, but the thought of having to go through this routine every day until we reached Moscow filled me with dread. I thenceforth resolved to shave only every other day. Back in the compartment, Vova grinned when he saw me, then began patting his cheeks vigorously.

Stuffing my shaving kit back in my suitcase, I sat down on the empty bottom bunk across from the Russian family. They were looking at me pensively now, almost sorrowfully, and I wondered what they were thinking. They seemed to regard me as some sort of oddity, as a creature from another world. God, I thought, this is punishing; like being in a cage, or a goldfish bowl: I'm traveling nearly a quarter of the way around the world with these people and there's nothing to do but sit and stare at each other. What's behind those shy, solemn stares, anyway? Do they loathe Americans because of what's happening in Vietnam? Or have they even heard of Vietnam? Vova seems civil enough, but the woman and child have not smiled at me once. Or at anything else, for that matter.

Leaving the compartment, I walked the entire length of the train, thinking I might run across my Japanese acquaintances. At least the Japanese spoke English. At least they would be someone to talk with.

It was to no avail. The Japanese seemed to have vanished. Or possibly they'd never even boarded. Perhaps they'd remained in Nakhodka, having had their schedules changed. It struck me then, with a sudden, almost frightening realization, that I must be the only Westerner—perhaps the only foreigner—on the entire train. Apparently no one else even spoke English.

I came back up the corridor, heading for the dining car. It was nearing eleven o'clock. At least in the diner I could smoke and watch the passing landscape without being stared at.

Entering the dining car, I was met by a jittery stewardess, who quickly began shaking her head, almost yelling, "*Nyetabyehd! Nyetabyehd!*" or something similarly unintelligible. I suspected she was advising me that I was too early for lunch, so I flashed my cigarettes and backed over to a booth in the corner. She followed me closely, her voice rising in pitch, and only with great effort was I able to make her see that I didn't expect to be served yet, that I only wanted to smoke and look out the window.

It was a good ten minutes before I realized what the stewardess was trying to tell me: we were pulling into station at Khabarovsk; we would shortly be leaving the train; no noon meal would be served. All this came to me as more and more track crossings and wooden bungalows began to appear outside the window, as the locomotive gradually reduced its speed and the outskirts of a large city began to take shape.

The train slowed even further. Brick and concrete warehouses replaced the paintless bungalows. I looked at the stewardess, who was feverishly polishing the tables and windows. "Khabarovsk?" I asked.

"Khabarovsk," she said, lifting an imaginary spoon to her mouth and pointing toward the window.

I returned to my compartment as the train squealed to a stop. The room was empty, but there was a burly, rock-faced official waiting for me in the doorway. "You will follow me," he said, dourly, and I did, grabbing my camera as we left.

Out on a wide, unevenly paved platform, the official kept looking around uncertainly, as though unfamiliar with the surroundings himself. "You will wait here," he said, finally. "Do not leave, please." He then disappeared back onto the train.

I waited for perhaps twenty minutes, watching a crew of females load baggage and listening to songbirds warble in the nearby trees. I felt impatient and helpless, but what else could I do? Not too distant from the station I could see blocks of stark, modern-looking office buildings, beyond which rolls of carbon-black factory smoke curled lazily into the sky. Walking across the platform, I asked two seedy-looking young men sitting on a bench if they spoke English, but they only shook their heads. When I managed to convey that I was an American, however, they began to show more interest. I offered them cigarettes, which they examined very carefully before accepting. Then each did a curious thing: one man reached in his pocket and handed me a large coin not quite the size of a silver dollar; the other took off the pair of aged plastic sunglasses he was wearing and placed them gently over my eyes. I was trying to think what to say or do next when I saw a slim, well-dressed woman moving briskly toward us on the platform. Seeing her coming, the two men hurried away.

"You are the American?" the woman asked when she came up, but she was obviously distracted by the men—whom she later described as "hooligans"—scurrying down the platform.

"Yes," I said, eagerly. It seemed months since I had heard someone speak clear English and almost immediately I felt reassured.

"I am your Intourist guide for this afternoon," she went on, in a musical, only slightly accented voice. "My name is Filia." By this time her dark green eyes were regarding me steadily.

We shook hands and I told her my name.

Filia was young (in her early twenties, I guessed) and strikingly attractive, with long, light brown hair neatly pinned up in back of her head. She wore gleaming gold earrings and a bright pink summer dress, which I thought looked slightly cool for the sixty-odd-degree weather.

After a polite exchange, she inquired, "Well, what would you like to do this afternoon? We have several hours before your train leaves."

I had no idea what there was to do on an afternoon in Khabarovsk, and asked for her suggestions.

"First," she said, glancing at her watch, "we should like to eat, I suppose," and when I agreed, we hailed a taxi and spun off toward town.

Near the middle of the business district we hopped out of the taxi and strolled along what Filia announced was Karl Marx Street, a wide, bustling thoroughfare laden with buses and army jeeps. We came at last to a small, open-air restaurant.

"This is my favorite," she said, proudly. "I hope you will like it also."

I said I was sure I would, and I did. We had sardines and potatoes and some highly seasoned but delicious spotted sausage, topped off by buttered brown cake and sparkling champagne.

Strangely, though, during the course of the meal we spoke very little. Filia, I soon discovered, was not exactly an effusive conversationalist, the majority of my comments and queries eliciting only short, sometimes one-word replies. For the most part she sat quietly, eating slowly and fastidiously, every now and then turning her soft, finely chiseled features to gaze toward the sidewalk.

As we were finishing our dessert, Filia glanced at me and said, "You seem displeased. Is there anything wrong?"

I looked at her curiously. "Displeased? No, of course not. I was just thinking about how far it is to Moscow. I'm not exactly looking forward to such a long ride." I was giving her a chance to assure me that it wouldn't be all that bad, but she only smiled and said, "Oh, but you will enjoy Moscow. It's such a fabulous city, you know."

"Have you ever been there?" I asked.

"No," she said, "but one day I hope to go."

Leaving the restaurant, we continued up Karl Marx Street, with its broad, tree-lined sidewalks, and crossed into the spacious Lenin Square where Filia pointed out a huge statue of the great revolutionary. Ancient-looking women and young children were reverently laying flowers at the foot of the monument. "You will see his real body in Moscow, yes?" Filia asked.

"Yes, perhaps," I said, thinking of the famed corpse lying permanently in state.

"Good," she replied, "and now we will catch a bus for some sightseeing."

Moving around the side of the Lenin statue, I caught another glimpse of the skyline above the downtown business district. While Khabarovsk had grown rapidly during its relatively short span of years, it seemed unusually symmetrical and well planned. Scores of five- and six-story apartment buildings, all nicely spaced, rose in every direction, and wide avenues, all clean and scrubbed-looking, divided the blocks of structures into neat, almost perfectly shaped squares. Despite such apparent perfection, however, the vista before me looked cold and uninviting. Somehow, I didn't think there would be that many sights to see.

"Do you like to walk?" I asked Filia.

"Walk? Yes, of course. I love to walk. Especially in a city like Khabarovsk."

I told her that if she didn't mind I would prefer walking to riding a bus since I had been riding for so long and had so much farther to go. I thought maybe if I tired myself out enough I would sleep away the first few days on the train.

She agreed and proved to be a very energetic, almost indefatigable walker. Over the next few hours we hiked briskly to what she considered were the important sights in downtown Khabarovsk—from the tombstone in Lenin Square (which marked the graves of soldiers killed in the 1929 Russo-Chinese conflict) to the Amur Sailors' Memorial (commemorating the seamen who died during the Revolution); then back down Karl Marx Street all the way to Komsomolskaya Square high above the swift-flowing Amur River. From here we could just see "the Tower," where a number of Hungarian and Austrian musicians were shot for refusing to play the imperial Russian anthem. From the square she also pointed out—in the far distance—the Civil War Victims' Memorial, under which she said was located the very ravine where, during revolutionary days, a host of barbaric executions took place.

"I would also like to take you to the Volochayevka Museum," Filia said, as we stood on the stone steps. "But I'm afraid we don't have time."

"What's at the museum?" I asked.

"It's a memorial," she replied, "to the heroes of the Battle of Volochayevka, a beautiful building over the graves of one hundred and eighteen soldiers who fell in the battle of 1922."

I said I was sorry we couldn't see it, but as I stood with her on those bare stone steps I was glad there wasn't time.

Already I was weary of walking and my feet ached profoundly; most of all, I was tired of seeing monuments to people who had died so violently. It was midafternoon now and the sun was at its brightest. The coolness of the morning had vanished (suddenly, it seemed) and it was becoming quite hot. Only on the steps had I begun to notice the heat, but the oppressiveness of the monuments to the dead I had felt everywhere, and at each one we viewed I imagined the anguished cries of the dying, frozen forever in grim, gray marble.

By the time we finished walking back up Karl Marx Street again the dry heat was simmering above the pavement. Trudging toward the station, I began to feel more and more like the proverbial wayfaring stranger. I was isolated, halfway around the world from home. I wished I had already arrived in Moscow. For that matter, I wished I were already back in America. I could foresee nothing for the next week but a continuation of the grueling monotony of the previous night's journey. It had been nice to get my feet on solid ground for a change, but the thought of boarding the train again had hung in the back of my mind all afternoon. It was ironic, too, I thought, because I had always relished train rides before. But all my other trips—through Europe and the American South—had been brief by comparison, and there had always been people to talk to.

Back at the railway station, Filia led me to my coach, then boarded the train and accompanied me to my compartment. There were numerous other passengers boarding now, struggling with odd-shaped bundles and string-tied boxes, bidding farewell to their friends and relatives with tearful kisses and many hugs, as if they might never see them again.

Pulling back the sliding door, I stopped in the doorway, looking around curiously. The coach was exactly where it was before, but somehow it seemed different. Glancing up, I saw my suitcase pushed back against the wall on the top bunk, but in a different position than I'd left it. And where were my compartment mates? I looked at the bunks opposite mine and saw several suitcases piled on the lower one. On the upper bunk were a number of small bundles and some boxes wrapped tightly with thick cord. I turned back to Filia. "This is not the same train," I said.

"No," she replied. "You always change trains at Khabarovsk; unless you are coming from Vladivostok. This is now the *Rossiya* Express. Or *Russia*, if you prefer."

"But how did my suitcase get here?" I inquired.

"It was moved for you," Filia laughed. "How did you think?"

"Oh," I said. "Yes. Of course."

We then heard a voice crackling through the public address system, at the conclusion of which message Filia warned me to pay strict attention. "You must always listen very carefully to these announcements," she said, earnestly.

I reminded her that I understood no Russian.

"It doesn't matter," she replied. "They are generally only to tell you that the train will be leaving shortly. You must listen very closely or you might miss the train."

"Of course," I answered.

"And now I must be going," she said, turning toward the corridor. She paused, looking back at me. "I wish for you very good luck—and also a pleasant journey."

As cool and distant as Filia had been, I felt a twinge of disappointment as she walked away. I was in the midst of a strange, unfamiliar land, without friends or any source of communication. However brief the acquaintance, she'd seemed like a small oasis in a boundless desert. As the train began pulling out I sat down wearily on the bottom bunk, a vision of thousands of miles of unbroken railway stretching before my eyes. I stepped to the nearest window, hoping to catch a last glimpse of Filia, or a last wave. I did see her, but she never turned. As the engine picked up speed, her figure receded in the distance and was blotted out finally by the whiz and blur of swiftly passing trees and buildings.

After the station vanished from view, I remained in the corridor watching rows of apartment complexes streak past the window, followed by blocks of plain, empty-looking warehouses and a huge, flame-belching oil refinery. Not long afterward, we crossed the majestic Amur Bridge—a marvel of steel-beam construction—and passed over the wide and mighty Amur River, which for hundreds of miles serves as the Sino-Soviet border, and which, according to Filia, rises up after storms and heavy rains to sweep away and devour entire villages, thereby earning its Chinese name—the Black Dragon.

We gradually entered a low, flat no-man's-land, dotted with lonely wild flowers, pale green ferns, and sprawling willows. In the distance, just over the southern horizon, rose the forbidding hills of northern Manchuria.

Sometime later, steeling myself against a gathering gloom, I went back to my compartment and climbed into bed. Already the movement of the train had made me drowsy, and the long afternoon walks had begun to have their effect. No sooner had I lain down than I sank into a deep and dreamless sleep.

I awoke to find the Russian family back in the compartment. Lodged comfortably in their bunks, they were staring at me silently through quizzical eyes. I was surprised to see them, having assumed they had gotten off at Khabarovsk, but very glad; and despite their stares, they seemed glad to see me. It struck me how easily time could be twisted by the passage of events: I had known these people less than twenty-four hours, yet now they seemed like old acquaintances, even old friends, despite the fact that my communication with them had been almost nonexistent. Aside from my suitcase, they were the only constants in a situation that was continually changing.

As I climbed down from my bunk, Vova was pointing to his watch, motioning me toward the door. I looked through the doorway, to the window on the other side of the corridor. The sun had already dipped below the horizon, leaving a cool, radiant sheen on what looked like ghost trees silhouetted in the twilight. What was he trying to tell me? I wondered, still trying to shake the cobwebs loose. Then I remembered. It was suppertime, of course. I should get to the dining car before it closed.

As I moved down the corridor toward the diner, something began gnawing at my memory. When I left the compartment, what was that lying on the bottom bunk? It was a suitcase, wasn't it? We must have a new compartment mate. I staggered on through the next coach, then the next, until I reached the dining car.

Inside the diner, I found a seat by the window and pointed out some items on the menu to the stewardess, still having no idea what I was ordering. Nearly half an hour later (I didn't mind the wait; there was nothing else to do at this hour), the stewardess brought me some chicken cutlets, a bottle of dry white wine, and a bowl of something I had eaten once before but had forgotten the name of. It looked like a kind of beet soup. "*Borscht,*" the stewardess said, when I pointed to it.

"Yes, *borscht,*" I repeated after her, trying to forget how it tasted.

After the meal, I remained in the diner as long as possible, smoking and trying to make a few notes in my journal. There wasn't much to write about, but the effort helped pass the time. When the stewardesses began to look impatient I returned to my compartment. As I entered the doorway, my eyes leaped to the suitcase on the bunk below mine. It was opened and pushed toward the far end of the bed. "So," I thought. "We *do* have another compartment mate." Vova and his family were all in bed, reading. When he saw me pondering over the suitcase, Vova began jabbering something, then pointed toward the corridor, apparently trying to tell me that our new companion, whoever it was, was down the hall somewhere.

The news of another roommate was not unwelcome; a new face would at least add a little variety to the compartment. Was it a man or woman? I wondered. I studied the suitcase more closely, but it was impossible to tell the sex of the owner. I looked back at Vova, wondering how to ask him. The obvious motions would have been a little awkward with his wife and child watching, so I tried to think of something else. Pointing to the suitcase, I put my hands just above my ears and ran them slowly down the sides of my face, trying to suggest long hair, but when I looked toward the three of them, they had rather puzzled expressions on their faces and were merely gazing back at me. It was obvious they had no idea what I was trying to convey. Suddenly, the discontents of the past few days seemed to overwhelm me. I felt frustrated, angry even. Well, dammit, I thought. I'll *make* them understand me. Even if it takes all night. Why not? There's nothing else to do on this godforsaken train. I tapped the suitcase again, this time emphatically, then pursed my lips and pretended I was putting on lipstick; then I licked each of my index fingers and ran them slowly over my eyebrows, slicking them back with the moisture.

The mother and little Yuri were still gaping at me, as if I had lost my senses; but Vova's face, though still puzzled, was beginning to show traces of a smile. I made as if to straighten my dress, then prissed my way to the window, bent over primly, and very daintily pulled back the curtains and peeked out.

When I turned back around, I was astonished to find them all smiling, Yuri especially. He was grinning broadly, nodding his head as if everything were now perfectly clear. When I attempted to speak in a high falsetto, my voice squeaked and Vova laughed out loud, then began frantically pointing to the suitcase, bobbing his head affirmatively, over and over.

With the question of our roommate's sex apparently resolved, I assumed that my demonstration was over; but Vova continued making motions, speaking out loudly and urging me on, his wife and Yuri still looking at me, smiling expectantly. Only gradually did it strike me that what they wanted was for me to go through the whole routine again, which finally I did (to their very obvious and vocal approval). Before they could persuade me to go through with it a third time, however, I excused myself and stepped out into the corridor, fearing that when I ran out of pantomimes we would lapse back into that hideous silence again. Just at that moment, though, I felt rather proud of myself and not a little pleased that I had finally managed to communicate something. "Well," I thought, moving on down the corridor, "at least I know I'm in with another one of my opposites."

A number of the compartments were open now, filled with people. On the way from Nakhodka to Khabarovsk the coach had seemed deserted, but now it was teeming with passengers, most of them chattering, drinking, smiling, and laughing. Their obvious enjoyment, however, made me feel all the more removed. I stopped at several of the doorways and peered in but everyone looked preoccupied; no one seemed to notice me, so I continued on down to the end of the corridor to a compartment that I guessed was the quarters of the conductor. Inside the room near the door was a large table around which three men were standing as if in a trance, watching two others absorbed in a game of chess.

One of the men watching wore a dark uniform and a shiny black cloth-and-plastic cap. He was, as I later learned, the *Russia*'s chief conductor (or *provodnik*, as they called him). When he saw me standing in the doorway he beckoned me in, but otherwise merely stood there watching the game, only occasionally glancing my way.

When the game ended I turned to leave, but the *provodnik* tapped me on the shoulder and with several simple gestures led me to understand I was being invited to play the next game.

"Me?" I said, surprised.

"*Da, da,*" the *provodnik* nodded. Turning to the group,

he announced, *"Amerikanets,"* and the group responded to the annunciation with curious, wide-eyed gazes. I wondered how he knew my nationality.

"No, no," I smiled, shaking my head. From what I had seen of the previous game, the men at the board had shown an expertise far beyond my own limited ability. I didn't want to be known as the great American dunce.

But the *provodnik* insisted. He turned toward the others, looking them over carefully, then singled out a red-faced, bulbous-nosed man. *"Da, vee,"* he said, tapping the man on the shoulder. It occurred to me he must be picking the most formidable player in the group to represent Mother Russia against the invading American in some sort of symbolic defense of the homeland.

I had played perhaps six games of chess in my life, none very recently, but from watching the previous contest, some of the more basic moves had begun coming back. Against my better judgment, I finally sat down and, trying to appear confident, lifted my king's pawn and audaciously moved two spaces ahead. My opponent, whose name I learned was Ivan, studied my move intently—as though I had done something unexpectedly devious. I assumed it was a rather standard opening, but in any case it was the only one I knew.

At length, Ivan moved his king's pawn ahead one space; and when I quickly moved my queen out four spaces, a chorus of grunts from the bystanders led me to suspect I was already in serious trouble. Studying the board more carefully, I began to realize just how imprudent my move was. Ivan would now come in quickly for the kill.

After prolonged study, however, Ivan moved his rook's pawn on the opposite side of the board. I breathed a quick sigh of relief, but the guffaws coming from the background aroused my suspicions. "Uh-oh," I thought. "He's setting me up for something; I'll have to be more cautious." I returned my queen to her original position, then looked up at the spectators, observing only pained, puzzled expressions.

After a good deal of jockeying for position, my situation deteriorated drastically. Once again my queen seemed inextricably hemmed in, and try as I might, I couldn't see a way out. An uneasy silence fell across the room, broken only by the moan of rolling wheels.

While I was contemplating my fate, a tall dark curly-haired young man, whose name I later learned was Felix, appeared in the doorway, and after some moments watching said something I guessed was, "Do you speak Russian?"

I shook my head and continued to stare at the board. A few minutes later, he asked, "*Sprechen Sie Deutsch?*"

"*Nein,*" I replied, without looking up.

"*Nein?*" he said; then laughed and began speaking rapidly, asking one question after another. Since I understood his query and answered in German, all so casually, he assumed I knew the language quite well, which I didn't. Several years before, I had picked up the rudiments of conversational German during a summer's stay in Berlin, but by this time had forgotten most of it.

Ignoring Felix's questions, I managed to salvage my queen, but a few minutes later was back in hot water again. Felix was now beginning to give me hints in German on which move to make, hints I only vaguely understood.

This time my queen appeared lost for certain, but I did have a few alternatives. Strangely, the onlookers appeared to be sympathizing with my situation. With curious head-shakes and eye movements the men standing behind my opponent began giving me subtle suggestions as to which move to make. Disregarding them, I finally extricated my queen but sacrificed a rook and a knight in the process.

Soon afterward, when I fell into yet another predicament, the same men began giving me suggestions that were far less than subtle. As Felix babbled in German, the others began making wild, frantic motions and pointing vigorously to the board; but they disagreed among themselves as to which was the proper move. Finally, one of the men pushed the other two aside and actually reached over and moved my rook himself, which precipitated a heated quarrel. When my opponent turned around to see what was going on, his arm brushed the table, knocking the board and all the pieces onto the floor, which nearly provoked an outright brawl. It was all Felix and the *provodnik* could do to separate the three of them.

There were no more chess games that night; but after the near free-for-all I stood at the doorway for a long while, trying to make sense of Felix's friendly chatter, finally piecing together what he was trying to tell me: Ivan was not a chess player either.

It was only later, however, when I was back in my bunk drifting off to sleep, that it dawned on me that what the *provodnik* had done was to deliberately select the *worst* player in the group as my opponent.

JULY 11— . . . *moving languidly now, through the endlessly rolling hills of the east Siberian uplands, ubiquitous silver birch trees drifting softly past my window. There must be millions, even billions, of them and sometimes it is difficult to tell whether we are passing them or they are passing us.*

Every fifty or a hundred miles we creep by a tiny cluster of brown wooden houses clinging vainly together in an effort to ward off the immense, seemingly oppressive solitude. Once in a great while we stop—for a minute or so—just long enough to take on a passenger or two, sometimes leaving one behind . . . then continue on, wending our way through a land that is remote, strangely beautiful, yet silent and unresponsive, like Filia.

We are still on the edge of Manchuria, looking southward, toward the hinterland of China and its nebulous interior. . . .

I awoke sluggishly that morning to an empty compartment, disappointed to realize that it wasn't very late. I had hoped to sleep away most of the morning, but I could tell by the position of the sun that it couldn't be too long past eight o'clock. After a futile effort to drift back into unconsciousness, I got up and staggered to the washroom, then returned to the compartment, wondering about the mysterious body I had brushed past on the bunk below mine the night before. The body and the Russian family were all at breakfast, I assumed. Feeling my face, I thought for a moment about shaving and remembered that just the previous morning I had vowed to shave only every other day. I decided to break the vow. At least the act of shaving would help chip away at the time. So I trudged on down to the washroom again and laboriously completed the task. Then I went on to the dining car.

Inside the diner, I looked for Vova and his family, but they were nowhere to be seen. I sat down at a table just inside the door and moved over next to the window, near a small vase of white velvety flowers, to get a better view of the countryside. The view was much the same as it had been the day before, the dominant impression being one of trees—endless miles of silvery-white birches standing mute and aloof like a vast throng of silent, lonely people. The train was creeping through the midst of the trees at a disheartening pace, sometimes less than thirty miles per hour. Why aren't we going any faster? I kept wondering. We'll never make it to Moscow at this rate. But we kept crawling along, as if some unseen, overpowering force were deliberately holding us back.

After I finished my breakfast, which consisted chiefly of a large meatball on buckwheat, I remained at the table awhile, hoping maybe somebody would stop by and sit down. I didn't care at that point whether they could speak English or not. A small stream of people continued to file in and out of the diner, but no one even looked my way. Finally, I turned back to the window, toward the trees, listening to the drone of sonorous music flowing from the public address system. As the train moved on, the dense forests occasionally gave way to solitary fields and meadows, and once to a broad, barren plain. Looking out, I had a sudden vision of Genghis Khan and his Golden Horde of Mongolian tribesmen thundering over the horizon. For a fleeting moment I imagined their wild and dusky faces straining toward the dining car above incredibly swift-moving horses. In reality, the speed of the train at this point was such that Khan and his horde could easily have overtaken us.

I had almost forgotten about our new roommate, but when I returned to the compartment there she was, resting on the edge of her bunk. I remembered at once having seen her leave the diner shortly after I entered. So, I thought: the mystery woman at last. She was sitting there calmly, with her legs crossed, as if she had been expecting me; a faint, friendly smile spread easily across her face.

"How do you do?" she said, warmly. "You must be the American."

"Yes, I am," I replied, surprised and elated that she

spoke English. I introduced myself and she said, "*Zhay...*," not quite getting the *J* sound. Then she told me she was a schoolteacher from Khabarovsk, that she was going to visit relatives somewhere this side of Moscow, and that her name was Tamara.

"Ta-MA-ra," I repeated, and she smiled broadly, revealing a gleaming set of evenly spaced teeth beneath a short crop of sandy-red, very curly hair.

A few minutes later Vova and his family came in, and for the first time I was able to learn something specific about them. I listened in fascination as Tamara related the details: Vova was a sailor by profession; he had lived all his life in Nakhodka, and was employed by the merchant marine. His wife's name was Natasha and their only son, Yuri, had just completed his first year in school. They were all going to Moscow for the first time, which for Vova and Natasha was to be the fulfillment of a life's dream.

We sat there talking for perhaps half an hour, Tamara serving as interpreter. For the most part, though, the conversation was subdued—friendly, but somehow less cheerful than the occasion seemed to warrant; informative rather than ebullient. There was one light moment: when Tamara told me that Vova and his family had believed the night before that I had already made her acquaintance and that I was actually doing an impersonation of her, rather than just an impression of a woman. Everyone grinned at that, but soon afterward a lull developed in the conversation—much sooner than I would have liked. Suddenly, there seemed nothing else to say. I began to feel despondent again, as though this small bit of brightness were merely an illusion. The whine of wind and wheels began to flood the silence, engulfing us in a deadening hum, and I got up to excuse myself. As I turned toward the doorway, Tamara asked, with a wry twinkle, "And how do you like the fast train *Russia?*"

"Oh," I said, pausing. "I like it fine." But as I walked on down the corridor I kept thinking, "fast train *Russia,*" wondering how anything moving as slow as thirty miles per hour could be referred to as a "fast train." Especially did it seem odd because I had ridden several trains in Europe and Japan at speeds over a hundred miles per hour. Fast train *Russia*, I mused. And the way she had said it—so proudly, as though she had helped build it herself.

I had been gone only a few minutes when I felt the *Russia* begin to slow even further, then further, and as if on signal the passengers on our coach began to emerge from their compartments into the corridor. Suddenly, instead of being alone, I was surrounded by thirty or forty people, most of whom were still in their pajamas. They were all grinning and chattering away in lusty, vibrant voices. I wondered what was going on as they brushed past me, crowding toward the exits at the ends of the coach.

In time I would learn to read the schedules in the foyers of the coaches—which, in the Cyrillic alphabet, told where and how long each stop would be—but for now I was in total ignorance. If we were making our first major stop, as I could only guess, I wanted desperately to get off the train; but having no idea how long we would be in station, I decided for the time being to stay put.

Even before the train came to a complete stop I noticed that many of the passengers had already leaped off. I was standing near the exit, watching from the window. Then, just as the locomotive ground to a halt, I felt a tug at my shoulder. Looking around, I saw Felix and the *provodnik*, whose name I shortly learned was Mikhail, motioning for me to follow them. I hesitated for a moment, then together the three of us stepped off the train onto the paved platform and headed toward a long row of shops and stalls.

Most of the main stations, as I was to observe, were clumps of sizable stone structures of prerevolutionary vintage, painted bright yellow or brown or white, with glistening tin roofs. There was usually an imposing poster portrait of Lenin on the office building nearest the tracks. "Skovorodino," Felix said, announcing the name of the town. He and Mikhail kept turning around making sure I was following them.

The platform was filled with people, only about half of them from the train, but practically all clad in pajamas and many wearing paper hats; a kind of reception party, it appeared. With Felix and Mikhail leading the way, we hurried through the stalls—*kioski*, they called them—browsing among the articles for sale, most of which were food items (onions, cucumbers, yogurt, bread, etc.), until we came to a place where Felix said, *"Morozhenoye!"* Ice cream! I reached for a ruble, but Mikhail shook his head and paid for the three of us.

It was quite tasty, this Russian ice cream. I had heard about it, and found that it was every bit as good as American ice cream. We got some peach-colored dips in paper cups and walked slowly back down the platform, through the crowds of people, eating with wooden spoons as we walked, and watching the engines being changed. Felix, with some difficulty in our mutually foreign language, made me understand that this engine change was the principal reason for our stopping at Skovorodino.

It was undeniably pleasant getting off the train like this and strolling along the platform. There was a casualness about the occasion that reminded me of a small country fair. Afterward, however, whenever I thought of such stops, the dominant memory would be of how prevalent were the women: in the kiosks they were hawking ice cream and fruit and vegetables; on the platforms they were operating beer wagons; in their carrot-colored fatigues they were toiling among the crossties. Even at the gate crossings female guards stood perpetually at attention in ironbound stances.

Fifteen minutes after the train stopped, the engine gave a sudden jerk and slowly began moving ahead. At the instant the locomotive lurched, my pulse quickened and I began looking for the door to our coach, but Felix and Mikhail never even flinched. Nor did any of the other passengers. "Hey," I said, looking around, "the train's leaving." But still nobody moved to get on. As the wheels began turning a little faster, I began searching for our coach more earnestly. "Hey," I almost shouted, looking back at Felix and some of the other passengers. "Isn't this our train?" Strangely, I began to think it wasn't—but what other train could it be? And if it weren't, why were the passengers walking toward it?

For a moment, it occurred to me that maybe everybody was getting off at this station.

No, that's absurd, I thought. I looked back around for Felix and Mikhail, but I couldn't see them anymore; they were lost in a maze of pajamas. Suddenly, as the train began picking up more speed, I felt a surge of panic, then desperately broke through a cluster of bystanders and started jogging along the platform, searching frantically for the door to our coach. I still couldn't find it, but finally leaped for the nearest coach anyway, wondering if I were making the right decision, fearing that maybe this was a different train after all.

When I got a firm grip on the hand railings, I turned around immediately and saw a curious sight: practically all of the remaining passengers, perhaps sixty or seventy of them, were jogging leisurely down the platform after the moving train, but they were still not getting aboard, even though the train was now rolling along at at least five miles an hour. What are they doing? I thought. What in God's name are they waiting for?

Not until the train was moving almost as fast as some of them could run, did the passengers begin leaping back on, one by one. "Get on, get on!" I shouted, "Jump!" and finally they all did—at the very last moment. Watching them board, I thought, What a strange game to play. But eventually everyone made it and I wondered why I had gotten so upset, since it couldn't have meant anything to me if any of them had been left behind. It occurred to me, though, that if this kind of thing went on at each and every stop some of the passengers were bound to be left, sooner or later, simply by the law of averages. Afterward, when I managed to express this concern to Felix, he merely laughed and said, "*Ja; ja, das ist recht.*"

Despite the uneasiness of the boarding incident, the excitement left me feeling a little more alive. In general, the stop had been refreshing and had helped break the monotony of the long morning's ride. But by midafternoon we had settled back into the old routine—creeping slowly along to the unbroken thrum of music and the endless vista of birch forests. Just before noon, a beautiful river—the Shilka, I was told—came quietly into view and the fast train *Russia* followed it faithfully the rest of the day, past little brown cabins with immaculate white curtains and cherry-red flowers in the windows.

Late in the day the vast wild and verdant land with its lonely, winding rivers began to change: the birch forests began to thin, disappearing finally in a dry, rocky wasteland as we skirted the fringes of the great Gobi Desert. Already it seemed that I had been on the fast train *Russia* for an eternity. We were still "only" a thousand miles out of Khabarovsk, and the incessant bumping and swaying engendered such a pervasive lethargy that it was all I could do sometimes to make it to the bathroom.

In the diner that evening I again ate alone. I kept looking around for Vova and his family, and especially for Tamara, but they never came in. Once more I was reduced to gazing out the window, with only the white velvety flowers for company. Once, a rather seedy-looking, baggy-faced man came by and sat down briefly and we downed some warm, flat beer together. He pointed to the flowers, raising his eyebrows as if to ask, You like? and I nodded. Beyond that we could communicate very little, and not long afterward he was gone.

When I got back to the compartment, Tamara was not there, nor was Natasha, but Vova was sitting on the bottom bunk playing a game of chess with Yuri. They seemed eager to have me join them and motioned for me to sit down. I watched their game for a while, and every now and then Vova or Yuri would glance up and grin. I kept looking around anxiously, hoping Tamara would come back, but she never appeared. Awhile later Natasha came in, dressed in her pajamas. She smiled at me very cordially, then got in her bunk behind Vova and began reading. Later on I played a game of chess with Yuri and he seemed very pleased with himself when he beat me.

As soon as the chess game was over I got up to take a stroll, but just as I turned around Tamara came in. She had been down the corridor most of the evening, she said, visiting friends, but now she was ready to change her clothes and go to bed. She got her pajamas from her

suitcase and went to the washroom, and when she returned we had a long conversation about her work as a
schoolteacher. She said she had been teaching in the
schools for nearly six years and enjoyed it immensely.
According to her, the profession of teaching was one of
life's highest callings. "That, and being a good communist," she added.

When I asked if she spanked her children very much,
she looked horrified. "No, of course not," she said.
"There is no need to deliberately inflict pain on children."

"But what if they get out of hand?" I asked.

"Out of hand?" She seemed puzzled by the phrase, but
when I explained it, she said thoughtfully, "No, none of
my children ever gets out of hand. I cannot imagine that
ever happening."

Looking at the soft, radiant warmth of her face, I
tended to believe her. It was a countenance, a bearing that
would captivate children as surely as it charmed adults.

Yet somehow I wondered. I wished we could understand each other better, and I expressed regret at not
knowing her native language.

"You must learn the Russian language," she said. "In
fact, everyone should learn it. It's a beautiful tongue, and
very expressive."

"I already know seven words," I answered.

At that she laughed and said, "Well, it's a beginning,
and tomorrow I will teach you some more."

"You will?" I asked, surprised that she would offer.

"Of course," she said. "Because that's what I am—a teacher."

A few minutes later, I left the compartment and took a walk down the corridor for a late-night smoke before turning in. I stood at the window for perhaps half an hour, taking deep drags from my cigarette and peering through the glass at the pale white moon.

JULY 12—*Today we rose early, the day dawning to a still semidesert landscape, with Manchuria and Mongolia well to the south of us. This morning seems different than any other day, because all of us (Vova's family and Tamara and I) went to breakfast together. We sat at the same table where I usually sit alone looking out the window, and laughed and joked together. I learned six new words of Tamara's language and Natasha said my pronunciation was quite good. Somehow, things seem to be picking up; today seems more exciting than the rest of the trip.*

When we got back to the compartment, Tamara said, "And now I will teach you a new Russian word and a new card game, altogether at the same time. The name of the game is called *durak,* and it means 'fool.' "

"Durak," I repeated, and little Yuri clapped his hands, gleefully. *"Durak, durak,"* he said, apparently anxious to beat me at another game besides chess.

Durak turned out to be great fun, and with Tamara's help it was not difficult to learn the rules. But I quickly made a number of less than brilliant plays; some intentionally, so I could say after each such play, *"Ya* (I am) *durak"* (a fool).

Tamara laughed whenever I said, *"Ya durak,"* but Vova and Natasha would look at me sympathetically and shake their heads, saying (according to Tamara), "Oh, no. You are not a fool; oh, no, you are not." And I would grin back; but a little while later, after another such play, I would repeat the phrase and Natasha would put her hand on my shoulder and say, "Oh, no, you are not a fool. Really you are not." Tamara kept laughing through all of this, realizing I was only kidding, but Vova and Natasha remained ever sympathetic.

After an hour or so of *durak* I left the compartment and found some of the children from our coach playing in the corridor. There was one child named Olya, and another called Lenya; and one of the most beautiful little girls I had ever seen, named Nadya—a golden-haired six-year-old in a bright purple dress who had not yet lost her baby teeth. When Nadya smiled it seemed like the whole world was breaking out in brilliant sunshine.

And there was another child, eight or nine years old, a brown-haired girl with dark eyes and thin pale lips named Marina, who seemed painfully shy and reticent.

We played hide and seek in the corridor, and I pretended I was a monster. The children giggled and hid behind the curtains, and when I began talking through my cheeks like Donald Duck they squealed with delight and covered their faces. All except Marina, who watched coolly, almost somberly—then retreated quickly to her nearby compartment when I accidentally bumped against her.

Not too long before lunch the fast train *Russia* creaked to the morning's first major stop. We were at the old fur center of Chita, the junction for the former Chinese eastern line to Harbin and Korea. It was a smoky, dusty city with ashes floating in a grayish haze above rows of belching chimneys.

"Chita!" Tamara announced, coming out into the corridor. She and Vova took me by the arm, and with Natasha and Yuri close behind, we leaped off the train and went running down the platform toward the shops and stalls along the tracks.

The platform was crowded; even more so than at Skovorodino, and there seemed to be a greater variety of paper hats and pajamas. Tamara bought some black bread and oranges and two bags of nuts. She was standing there waiting for her change, the rest of us looking around for the ice cream stalls, when Felix and Mikhail came striding up. Mikhail suggested we go to a place he knew about two blocks away where he claimed (according to Tamara) the best ice cream in Siberia was served. But we would have to hurry, he said. Chita was only a fifteen-minute stop and there were perhaps eleven minutes left.

So we ran down the hill—the seven of us—as fast as we could travel, until we came to a small, ramshackle old hut. The front door was locked, and the shop seemed deserted, but Mikhail hustled around back and began pounding on the door. Moments later a sprightly, white-haired fellow loosened the front latch and ushered us up to a full counter of bright-colored flavors.

I reached for some rubles, but Vova motioned me away, paying the entire bill himself. I got vanilla and Tamara and the others got cherry, and polishing it off rapidly, we hurried back up the hill. Halfway up, Yuri stumbled and fell. I reached down quickly and hoisted him up on my shoulders and we continued on, laughing all the way to the platform, where the train was just beginning to pull out. Once again the passengers were running alongside the train, waiting until it picked up speed. This time I wasn't so apprehensive: it seemed thrilling now to sprint down the platform, waiting until the last possible moment to leap back aboard—and doing it myself, I understood why: it was to make the most of every second on solid ground.

Back on the train, Felix and Mikhail followed us to our compartment, where Tamara opened up the bags of nuts she had bought. We sat around munching the nuts and gaily rehashing our little escapade, before Mikhail was forced back to his duties. Conversing in German with Felix was proving difficult, but with Tamara's help I discovered that he was a mechanical engineering student in his last year at the university in Khabarovsk, and that he was going to Moscow to visit an older brother. Somehow I couldn't quite picture Felix as an engineering student; in any case, after the nuts were all gone, he followed Mikhail down the corridor.

After Felix left I played another game of chess with Yuri, and was beaten again. We then played some more *durak*, and Tamara taught me some Russian words: *kogda?* (when?), *spichki* (matches), and *univermag* (department store). After that I climbed up into bed and wrote down all the Russian words I could remember in my journal, coming up with a grand total of thirty-seven.

After lunch I walked down to the *provodnik*'s quarters at the far end of the coach, where Felix and Mikhail and several other men were huddled around a table listening to a high-pitched, fast-talking voice on Radio Moscow.

"*Lieben Sie der Futball?*" Felix asked me.

"Football?" I said. Then I remembered the World Cup games in England and how everyone except Americans referred to soccer as football. I told Felix I liked the game, but didn't know much about it. An American team had entered, but had quickly been eliminated by Mexico. I predicted Brazil would win because they had not been beaten since 1954.

"*Ja*, Brazil," Felix said, "*und* Pelé." He then told me

that Brazil had just beaten Bulgaria two to nothing, but that the Soviet Union was winning, too—against North Korea—and the Soviet Union, he was certain, would eventually win the cup.

I sat and listened to the rest of the game amidst boisterous shouting, as Russia defeated North Korea three to nothing. "Pelé, *ja,*" Felix kept saying, "*aber* Malofeev, Chislenko, *und* Lev Yashin, *auch!*"

Toward the early afternoon the landscape began to change. We were climbing away from the Gobi Desert area and the low Mongolian hills with their thornbushes and finely formed cedars, into craggy, rocklike country, and it soon became apparent that we were rapidly ascending into more mountainous terrain. Toward midafternoon we made a stop at Yablonovo to take on a new engine, then began a long climb into the Yablonovy mountain range, which has summits up to nine thousand feet. The air became noticeably cooler and the tracks began to wind more sharply. Frequently, I could see the engine ahead of us, weaving like a serpent's head as we chugged along.

When we got to Mogzon, Tamara and Vova and I jumped out and ran down the platform, but this stop was to be very brief. We barely had time to pick up some sweet rolls and donuts and hop back aboard. Back in our compartment, our attendant, Ilya, served us tea and we sat around talking and eating our pastries. Then, with the pastries and tea under our belts, Tamara began another lesson in Russian.

On through the late afternoon the train continued to wind and creep upward through the small towns of Kharagun and Khilok and Kushenga until finally we approached the old town of Petrovsk-Zabaikalskii, site of a huge metallurgical plant. As we reached the station, there was intense excitement among the passengers of our coach, and they began surging toward the exits even more quickly than usual.

"Come on, come on!" Tamara cried. "This is something you must see. Come quickly!" We leaped off the train and began running down the platform. All the passengers were hurrying to the far end of the station. I didn't quite know what I was running for, or to, but it felt good to be on firm ground again. Hastening along, I saw little golden-haired Nadya, who had apparently gotten separated from her parents. I reached down quickly and picked her up, then rode her on my shoulders the rest of the way to the station building, where a crowd was gathering, gaping at something and oohing and ahing. Moving up closer, still holding Nadya on my shoulders, I could see some large sculptures projecting from a background of stone—bas-reliefs of what looked like bearded Russian soldiers. I was standing there gaping with the others when Tamara came up and informed me that these were memorials to the officers who had rebelled against the czar many years before the Revolution, and who had been exiled to this place in Siberia. She called out the names of Bestuzhev and five or six others—the last survivors of the famed Decembrists.

"Oh," I said, wondering aloud how something so simple as a few bas-reliefs could excite such feeling in so many people.

"It is because," Tamara said, "they suffered so long and so hard with no recognition in their own lifetime trying to create a better world for us all that we must remember them; and because no one should ever forget those who sacrificed their lives for humanity. You yourself would come to cherish their memory if you could know, if you could feel how they had suffered."

"Yes, perhaps so," I replied. We stood there looking at the cold, finely hewn stone for several minutes; then I put Nadya down, just as her parents came up. Hugging Nadya, they smiled warmly, rewarding me with generous pats on the shoulder. As we began walking down the platform, Nadya grabbed my hand and toddled alongside me until we got to the coach.

Back on the train, we eased out of Petrovsk-Zabaikalskii with dense forests all around, and spent the rest of the day and into dusk riding on a high plateau—the steppes of Buryatia.

Shortly after we settled back in our compartment, Nadya's parents dropped by to bring me an apple. Little Nadya appeared with them at the door, smiling radiantly. I cupped my hands together and blew a tune through my fist. It wasn't exactly Tschaikovsky, but Nadya laughed in delight and urged me to play another one, which I did. Then they moved on.

"They are beginning to talk about you," Tamara said

to me, after Nadya and her parents left.

"Who's talking?" I asked.

"The other passengers on the coach. They are asking a lot of questions about you. I think they were afraid of you at first."

"Afraid of me?" I said. The remark sounded ludicrous, considering the fact that I was alone—the only foreigner on the train—unable to communicate with anybody except Tamara. "But they're not afraid anymore?" I asked.

"No," Tamara laughed. "I think it is because they have seen that you like children—and anyone who likes children must not be so terrible after all."

"Well, I'm glad they're no longer so frightened," I said.

"And after dinner tonight, I will take you to meet them all."

True to her promise, when we returned from the dining car that evening, Tamara took me by the hand and said, "And now let us visit some of our friends." Leading the way, she stopped by the compartment next to ours, where the little boy named Lenya was sitting next to the window. As soon as we walked in, I spoke to him in Donald Duck language and he giggled softly. The rest of the passengers laughed out loud.

"This is Mr. Zhay," Tamara announced. "He is an American—a teacher on his way to Moscow."

They all nodded and one woman said something, which Tamara translated as, "Yes, we know; you must sit down with us, please."

And so we sat down and talked for a while, and laughed

and drank some sherry, and when we left, the woman who had done most of the talking said, "You must always come see us again, because we are your friends forever." I thanked the woman and her companions for their sentiments, and also for their sherry, and then, at their request (for word spread rapidly on this train) I played another tune on my fist, which brought howls of laughter and a cheery round of applause.

Leaving their compartment, we went on to another, and then another, always receiving the same cordial welcome, and always partaking of something to drink. By the time we finished visiting all nine compartments, I was quite thoroughly soused. Even my whistling was coming out in a slur.

As a result, the last part of that evening seems very hazy and blurred, the sharpness of its memory being lost in a swirl of smiles and handshakes and laughter and drink. When Tamara finally led me back to our compartment, I crawled in my bunk and fell asleep; not, however, before making a few notes in my journal (entries that the next morning made very little sense to me). One thing I remembered clearly, however, was glimpsing in one of the middle compartments the dark-haired little girl named Marina, huddled against her mother near the window, peering at me, as before, through solemn, inquiring eyes.

JULY 13—*We are now not too far from Ir-kutsk, I believe. Tamara and Vova and his family have gone back to sleep, but I can't seem to manage it, even though I'm still a little woozy from last night. Instead, I'm taking advantage of the opportunity to make a few entries in my journal, something I haven't had much time to do the last day or two. . . .*

We seem to be following a small but beautiful river that no one knows the name of. The sun is hovering just above the treetops toward the east and sometimes the river comes clearly into view then suddenly vanishes, only to reappear around the next bend. . . .

Several hours before I wrote the above, I was awakened by a vigorous tapping on my shoulder. When I finally roused myself, Vova was pointing out the window, saying, "Baikal! Baikal!" I looked out blurry-eyed at a massive body of water, not realizing what it was until Tamara explained that this was the famous Lake Baikal—"sea," she called it—the oldest and deepest lake in the world. It was still dark, but there were lights along the shore, strung out evenly beside the tracks. Everyone on the train was up and looking out.

The "sea" seemed bleak and mysterious in the gloomy predawn hours and I remembered what I had long ago read in the books: how thirty million years ago cataclysmic tremors convulsed the middle of Asia, rupturing the land, heaving up giant mountains around a huge crevasse several miles deep; how through eons of time the crevasse filled with water, leaving a lake hundreds of miles long with myriad species of exotic plant and marine life (many of which exist nowhere else on earth)—diminutive blue seals and outsized sturgeons and transparent oilfish that melt away in the sun.

Looking out at the dark waters, I thought, What a fine refuge for monsters! Surely there must be legends here to rival Nessie or Bigfoot or even the Abominable Snowman. I was not disappointed: Tamara described a wraith-like, two-headed creature, half shark and half dragon, that slithered up from the sea's bottom only once a year—to feast on bears and wolves. And Vova told of an ancient mammoth with razor-sharp tusks and ivory hooves, which devoured anything moving, and which still patrols the northern shores of the lake at night, guarding against further encroachment of its domain by man.

Fantastic stories though they were, in Siberia they seemed much more believable, or at least less subject to ridicule. In this land of mountains and deserts and mighty rivers and lakes as big as seas, everything seemed larger than life. And so it was that morning, with the most spectacular sunrise I had ever seen. For nearly two hours, the *Russia* hugged the side of Lake Baikal, with wisps of fog to the north of us and jagged mountains to the south. Far away in the filmy offing, snowy peaks rose majestically, their delicate lines hardly discernible to the eye. And then, just as it must have appeared there for millions of years, a great corona of fire reared above the trees around the iridescent sea; the fog fled softly across the waters, and through the vanishing mists the ancient sun came smoldering, rising relentlessly above the far horizon, as if being lifted by the giant hand of God.

We cut through magnificent mountain scenery on the lake's southern side, past narrow, sparkling beaches and bold cliffs, with ridges of larch and cedar sweeping sharply into summits, then followed a lonely winding river along its course. By breakfast time we were pulling into the station at the large and famous city of Irkutsk.

"We will eat at the station this morning," Tamara said, just before we stopped. "Everybody off now."

When the train jangled to a halt, we hurried down the platform in the crisp morning air, the sunlight breaking through the musty buildings, bathing the ever-present Lenin poster in a cool red glow.

"We will be here for a long time," Tamara said, looking around at the station's concourse. Stopping at one of the tables, we ordered some sausage and bread and hot tea.

"How long will that be?" I asked.

"Seventeen minutes," she said. "It's the longest stop we make on the entire journey—because here we will get a change of linens and towels and the diner will be restocked."

It did seem like a long time compared to the other stops, most of which lasted less than ten minutes. Just as we were finishing our breakfast, a number of passengers from our coach—many of whose faces I remembered from the night before—came up and crowded around the table. They seemed glad to see me, and several of them patted me on the back and offered me food. One in particular, I noticed, was a short, slightly built fellow about fifty years of age, with slicked-back blond hair and a rough, craggy look. I thought he might have been a migrant worker or factory hand. He seemed especially interested in making my acquaintance, but before Tamara could introduce him, the train began pulling out and the group hastened back aboard.

I didn't see this man for the rest of the morning, but after lunch, after Tamara and Vova had gone back to the compartment, and while Felix and I were still sitting in the diner, he came up and sat down across from us at the table. He didn't say anything at first; he just sat there, smelling the flowers and every now and then touching them gently with the tips of his fingers. After a while, he began talking with Felix, and from Felix I learned that he was quite a renowned surgeon, known to all the passengers from Khabarovsk as "Dr. Viktor."

Later that afternoon, as we began to move deeper into the fabled Taiga (the Siberian forest known in summer as the "Blue Taiga" due to the smoky blue-green hue imparted to it by the pervasive larch trees), we made another stop—a short one this time—and Dr. Viktor, as soon as we jumped off the train, took some chalk from his pockets and hastily drew some lines on the pavement of the platform. Tamara and Felix and I were just behind him, watching closely. Then, along with Lenya and Olya and several of the other children, we began playing a Russian version of hopscotch. Dr. Viktor led the game off, followed by Tamara and Olya and then Felix. I didn't quite catch all the rules at first, so I kept missing my steps. Once, I was so off-balance that I toppled over on the pavement, coming to rest in a sitting position. Seeing me sprawled on the pavement with a fatuous grin on my face, the children began laughing and clapping their hands. Tamara and Dr. Viktor came over and helped me up, Tamara with a smirk on her lips, obviously suspecting I had exaggerated my imbalance.

"Why did you do that?" she said, grinning.

"Because," I said. "*Ya durak.*" And the children howled with laughter.

Back on my feet, I glanced toward the train and saw

the girl named Marina standing by her mother near the door to our coach. She was watching us closely, as though she would have liked to join us. I went over and tried to make her see that she could have a turn, too, if she wished. She seemed to understand what I was saying, but drew back warily, leaning closer against her mother.

"Your turn again!" Tamara yelled at me. "Your turn!" So I ran back over and took another turn as the train jerked and slowly started to pull away. Just before I finished, I glanced back toward the coach and saw Marina stepping up to the door, clutching her mother's hand. It was only then I noticed that she walked with a pronounced limp.

Running down the platform after the quickening train, I had a peculiar feeling in the pit of my stomach. I'd never noticed Marina's limp before because I'd never seen her take more than a few steps. Hurrying along the tracks, with Tamara crying, "You'd better get on! You'd better jump!" I kept seeing that faltering walk, those awkward little legs moving hesitantly across the pavement.

Back in our compartment, Tamara and Vova and I played a few rounds of *durak* and then I played another game of chess with Yuri. But I did so with little concentration. I kept thinking about Marina: how she'd never yet said a word to me, and how until now I'd never suspected the reason for her shyness. Strangely, I felt guilty and ashamed. No child should be crippled, I thought. They should all be robust and lively and able to play hopscotch. I thought about children in other parts of the world who were shy and lonely and, perhaps worst of all, who were living without hope or promise of happiness.

I mulled all this over for a long time. In my distraction I finally lost my queen and once again was checkmated. I stepped into the corridor and stared out the window, past the moving fields and forests. Sensing a change in my mood, Tamara came up behind me and stood for a moment, then gently placed her hand on my arm and said, "Don't feel bad; you are not a fool. Next time maybe you will save your queen."

Smiling, I turned around slowly and touched her cheek. "It's all right," I said. "Thanks for your sympathy." Then I went back inside and climbed into my bunk and drifted off to sleep.

From the diner that evening I saw a dazzling Siberian sunset, then remained at my table, smoking, watching the shadows creep across the land and the scattered farmhouses. We were still in the high country, gradually making our way down onto the long central Siberian plateau. The fleeting light gave an eerie sheen to an apparently illimitable expanse of green-hued forests, cut occasionally by fields heavy with violets and dewberries—in all, the land appeared to be a wild, incorporeal blending of immutable natural forms. It was a fitting end, I thought, to a day of awe-inspiring scenery.

A little after dark, Tamara came in with Vova and Natasha and a young woman named Lyuda from another coach. Lyuda, a pert, long-haired brunette, brought a sketchbook with her, on which she hastily penciled my portrait and handed it over, autographed, with an inscription, which Tamara translated: "For the American who calls himself a fool but who is our friend." I thanked Lyuda for the portrait, then borrowed her sketchbook and drew one of her, which I also signed and inscribed; and when Tamara read the inscription—"To a pretty friend from a friendly fool"—Lyuda blushed and shook her head sweetly.

After that, we ordered a round of beers and took turns drawing one another's portraits in the sketchbook and inscribing them with silly sayings. Beneath the picture Tamara drew of me, she wrote, "I'm going to bite you," which seemed a little odd. She had often said that over the past several days; whenever I began teasing her, as I frequently did, she would grin at me mischievously, waggling her finger and saying, "If you don't watch out, I'm going to bite you." It was only later that same evening, after we'd downed a few more beers and Tamara had asked me quite seriously if American teachers really bite their pupils that we realized, almost simultaneously, that all along she'd been confusing *bite* with *beat*. We had a hearty laugh over that, but Tamara had a difficult time explaining to Felix and Lyuda what was so amusing.

JULY 14—*All morning long the great Siberian plain has been unfolding its manifold treasures, its myriad foliages, lakes, and streams. Despite the changes in landscape, some of which have been remarkably abrupt, the persistent impression is yet one of tangled forests and winding dirt roads, of isolated farmhouses and gently sloping fields of windswept grass . . . a timeless terrain, immense and inscrutable. . . .*

Very early we crossed the mighty Yenisei River, stopping briefly at the large industrial city of Krasnoyarsk, where Lenin once paused on his way into exile. Hardly anyone was awake when we stopped, and I raised up only long enough to find out where we were, then went back to sleep.

After breakfast, Dr. Viktor dropped by for a few games of chess, but the good doctor proved to be a master and the games were embarrassingly brief. After he left, I took on little Yuri again and finally managed to win a game from him. In the three games we had played in the days before, I had only been half trying. On this occasion I decided to see if I could really beat him. I didn't succeed the first time, but on the second attempt I knuckled down and won. It was a mistake, however: I hadn't realized how competitive Yuri was. After he lost, he seemed very distraught, which prompted me to suggest we play another game. He refused, so I left for a stroll down the corridor.

Returning a few minutes later, I asked him again if he would like a rematch. This time he seemed eager to accept the challenge, and concentrating hard, I tried to make certain of two things: first, that it would be a close game (which it was); and second, that in the end Yuri would win (which he did). When he finally called checkmate, I pretended to be quite disgusted with myself and Yuri beamed with satisfaction. He tapped me on the hand, making motions to indicate that I'd played a good game and wishing me better luck next time.

Shortly after the last game ended, Ilya came in with tea

and biscuits, and soon after that Felix and Mikhail came by to listen to the latest round of the World Cup finals. Over warm, flat beer we heard Chile lose to Italy two to nothing and Portugal whip Hungary three to one. When Portugal scored its final goal, a groan of disappointment went up over the entire coach. As did Felix and Mikhail, most of the other passengers got very steamed up when following these games. They reeked with as much pride when boasting of their football team as they did when describing the exploits of their astronauts: Chislenko and Yashin were as heroic to them as Yuri Gagarin.

After the soccer matches were over, Olya, Nadya, and Lenya appeared at our door, giggling and babbling something that Tamara translated as: "Miss Tamara, can Mr. Zhay come out to play?" Tamara and especially Felix laughed loudly at this, the more so when I said to Tamara, "Yes, may I please go out to play, Mama?"

"Yes, Mr. Zhay," teased Tamara. "You may go out and play but don't stay too long." When I got up to leave, she shook her finger and added, "And don't forget to come back and wash your hands before lunch."

"I won't forget, Mama," I said, which drove them nearly into hysterics. From then on, I frequently referred to Tamara as "Mama."

Out in the corridor, the children and I played a version of blind man's bluff. I was the blind man and anyone I touched was "caught" and had to go back to "Mama" until everyone had been made prisoner. I put a handkerchief over my eyes and tottered forward like a zombie. I could hear the children squealing and scattering as I stalked down the corridor after them. Lenya hid behind a chair near the exit, but I cornered him quickly and sent him on to Tamara. The others ran on down the corridor. I finally caught Olya behind a curtain, but Nadya and Yuri and some of the others hid inside the compartments. I felt my way down the corridor, tapping on the compartment doors until I found one open. Stepping inside, I thought I heard Nadya giggling. When the grownups in the compartment saw me staggering in the doorway, they stopped talking; there was a long silence, then they began snickering, softly at first, then louder. As the laughing increased, I moved slowly in the direction of Nadya's giggle, then reached out my hand, groping, and felt it come to rest on another hand—but the hand was too large for Nadya's. I stopped, slowly removed my blindfold, and saw Lyuda looking back at me, profoundly astonished.

By then everyone in the compartment was shaking with laughter and the remainder of the children except Lenya and Olya were all at the door, snickering along with them.

"Ooh, me," I said, just as the train began to break its speed, "*ya durak,*" and they laughed still more.

"Oh, no," I guessed some of the adults were saying, "you are not a *durak,*" before the train slowed further and began grinding to a stop—at which point all of us dropped everything and scrambled for the exits.

Heading down the corridor, I heard a voice behind me crying, "Meester Zhay! Meester Zhay!" I turned around quickly and saw Lenya looking up at me. I knew what he wanted, so I reached down and lifted him up on my shoulders and we jumped off the train and hurried down the platform, surrounded by the rest of the children, hopping and skipping along gleefully. Looking around for Tamara, we headed for the nearest ice cream stall. Just before we got there, Tamara came running up beside us. Lenya wanted to go to her, so I put him on "Mama's" shoulders just as Olya ran by, begging to be lifted up. I hoisted Olya up, and after we got some ice cream Olya switched to Tamara's back and Yuri got on mine. Before the train started rolling again I had shouldered all eleven children from our coach—all except Marina—down the platform, sometimes doing deep kneebends as well, and skipping around in circles with some fancy dance steps thrown in. Once, toward the end of the stop, I caught a glimpse of Marina walking slowly with her parents. I started to go ask if she wanted to ride, too, but time was running out; the train was already beginning to move along and we had to sprint to catch up with it, once again leaping on board at the last moment.

Back in our compartment, I sat down wearily on Tamara's bunk, trying to catch my breath. The deep kneebends and the final dash for the train with Nadya on my back had left me thoroughly winded. Most of the children followed me inside, and the remaining half-hour before lunch was spent making pen sketches of each of them on scraps of paper from Tamara's notebook.

After lunch, I was looking forward to making a few

more entries in my journal and then stretching out on my bunk for a long, much-needed nap; but as soon as we returned from the diner, Tamara announced, "And now we shall go visit some friends in the hard-class section." By "hard class" she meant the coaches toward the front of the train, which were not quite as comfortable and a bit more crowded than those in our "soft-class" section. I had been through this section before, on two occasions: once, strictly from curiosity, when I first boarded the train, and once, merely to pass the time, just outside of Khabarovsk. On those occasions, when I hardly knew a soul on board, I was met only by dry, enigmatic stares from those who somehow must have guessed I was a foreigner but didn't know quite what to make of it.

The "hard-class" section consisted of wooden seats and bunks, and there were no private compartments. Passengers here purchased their food at stations along the way and rarely, if ever, came to the diner. Conditions were quite a bit more informal, with heaps of tattered packages and bundles piled in corners and against the windows. When Tamara and I walked in, a general lethargy was evident among the occupants: some were asleep on blankets on the floor in between the seats and bunks, and even in the aisles; most were sitting around smoking, knitting, or staring out the window and listening to the music from Radio Moscow, which seemed a bit louder in the stuffier atmosphere. Our presence seemed to stir them, slightly at first, then more perceptibly. As we walked toward the far end of the coach, where tea and biscuits were being

served, they rose and crowded around us, Tamara pausing along the aisle to greet several women she seemed to
know.

Toward the middle of the coach we passed a man in a
frayed brown army tunic with patches of faded red on his
collar. He was sitting near the window gazing into space
when we first walked in, but when he spotted me, he rose
immediately. I had seen him before, I remembered—the
second time I went through the coach. This time he
looked at me as though he knew me, grinning broadly,
showing a mouth of gleaming gold teeth. He was leaning
heavily on a crutch (one of his legs having been taken off
at about the knee), and he had only one hand, the side of
which he kept putting to his throat and shouting, *"Geet-
ler, kaput! Geet-ler, kaput!"* excitedly, with an expression
of almost unrestrained joy. I vaguely recalled his having
made similar gestures before, but at that time I was too
far away to hear what he was saying. Now he was almost
upon us, still crying, *"Geet-ler, kaput!"* Quickly, I looked
toward Tamara, seeking some explanation, and she
turned around to face him just as he hobbled up. I thought
for a moment he was going to hug us both, but for the
life of me I couldn't figure why. He stood there, spurting
out sentences broken with occasional grunts and shaking
my hand forcefully as the rest of the passengers began to
crowd closer.

After several uncertain exchanges, Tamara attempted
to explain the man's behavior: his name was Sergey; he
was a veteran soldier—a cossack, who'd suffered his

wounds while attacking Hitler's tanks on horseback. In the last days of the war, he had fought alongside the Americans in eastern Germany, helping to put the finishing touches to the Nazis—just before a grenade blew away his hand and leg. Sent home to a remote village in Siberia, he eventually recovered, but since those glorious days when he was in the full rush of manhood he had not seen an American; he had not laid eyes on a single one of his former comrades in battle. Seeing me now he somehow associated me with the great patriotic victory, with the climactic moment of his life, and he was overcome with emotion. He stood there, trembling, and finally stopped pumping my hand. For him, there was no Cold War, no bitter rivalry between America and the Soviet Union; there were only those *old* days when Americans and Russians were together against the dreaded Nazi juggernaut.

If it was an emotional moment for the old cossack, it was rather awkward for me. I didn't quite know what to say. I stood with my hands in the pockets of my jacket —the same jacket I'd worn while scaling Mount Fuji in Japan several weeks before. As I stood there, my fingers felt a sharp metal object—a souvenir medal that a Japanese guide had given me for climbing to the mountain's third station. Taking out the souvenir, I studied it for a moment. It wasn't much of a medal, but I pinned it on the old cossack's tunic and asked Tamara to tell him I was presenting it to him in memory of the Russians and Americans who once fought together against Hitler. By that time every passenger on the coach had closed up around us and when Tamara announced what I had said, a resounding shout rang out from the crowd. Visibly stunned, the cossack froze, then gripped me with a bear hug and stood there proudly, smiling through glistening eyes, while Tamara and I moved slowly back through the passengers toward the entrance of the coach. As we stepped through the doorway, I turned back once more and waved. The passengers were still roaring their approval, still waving and grinning. It seemed as though someone had turned up the music as loud as it would go. The old cossack was still swinging his hand against his throat and shouting, "*Geet-ler, kaput! Geet-ler, kaput!*"

*Over an hour has gone by since we returned
from the hard-class section, but I'm still sitting here with my ears ringing, still a little
numb from the experience. Tamara has told
everybody on our coach what happened, describing the affair in graphic detail. My
God, I feel like some kind of celebrity. . . .*

*We are now crossing the famous Ob
River, having just left the large industrial
city of Novosibirsk. Tamara says that
Novosibirsk is the greatest city in Siberia—
the economic and cultural center—but just
passing by, it seems but an afterthought.
Somehow mere cities don't seem so important
in a land where even the greatest are but dots
upon the universe. . . .*

I had sunk back on my bunk, intending to take only a short nap, but I must have been wearier than I thought and slept right through supper. When I awoke, Tamara was standing by me, smiling.

"What time is it?" I inquired.

"It's nine o'clock," she said. "Everybody was asking why you didn't come to the dining car."

"I wish I had," I said, sitting up on the edge of the bed. "Why didn't you wake me up?"

"We talked about it," Tamara said, "but you looked so peaceful we decided to let you sleep."

It struck me that I might be spending the rest of the night on an empty stomach.

"But don't you worry. Vova is making a cucumber salad for you."

I looked down at Vova on the other side of the aisle. He was energetically cutting up cucumbers and mixing the slices with shredded carrots and lettuce.

"That's very thoughtful," I said, sliding down onto the floor. I was as hungry as a horse.

"You can sit on my bed while I go to the washroom," Tamara said, and she left the room.

I sat on the edge of Tamara's bed, feasting on Vova's salad, every now and then looking up, saying, "Uhmm —delicious." Vova and Natasha watched me approvingly.

While I was eating, Nadya and Olya and some other children I'd never seen before appeared at the door, asking for Tamara. I pointed them down the corridor and they left. A few minutes later they reappeared, asking the same question, then vanished again.

A little while later Tamara came back from the washroom, looking fresh as one of the flowers from the diner. She had on a pair of bright pink pajamas and her hair was all fluffed up and shiny, still a little damp.

"The children have been looking for you," I told her.

"Oh?" she asked. "What did they want?"

"They just wanted to see you," I answered.

"They'll be back," she said, "and perhaps when they come we will sing some songs."

A few minutes later Nadya and Olya returned, followed shortly by Lenya and another child named Grisha. For nearly an hour we sang some bouncy folk songs that Tamara taught us and clapped to the beat of the music, the children's voices rising at times in perfect unison. I could only hum the tunes, of course, and clap along with them; but every now and then I would miss the beat and Tamara would tap my wrists, looking menacingly in my direction—at which time I would make a face back at her, waggling my finger and saying, "I'm going to bite you," which would make Tamara laugh—and whenever Tamara laughed, the children would break out in a fit of giggles.

Later, after the children went back to their compartments, Ilya served up some tea and biscuits and Felix and Mikhail came by with the latest sporting news: Brazil had been upset by Hungary, which moved the Soviet team farther up in the standings. Felix was ecstatic. Then

Lyuda and Dr. Viktor dropped in and we spent the remainder of the evening playing tic-tac-toe, which, surprisingly to me, they had never even heard of before.

Just after midnight we made a short stop at a small, seemingly deserted station. By this time most of the passengers on our coach were already asleep, but despite the late hour we decided to jump off and stretch our legs. The *Russia* had been making excellent time that day, moving over the flattening terrain at speeds exceeding fifty miles per hour, but the stops had been fewer than on other days and we felt a little more cramped than usual. So, thinking perhaps a late-night stretch would help us sleep better, Tamara and I and Felix and Mikhail and Lyuda and Dr. Viktor leaped off the train and made a quick run down the platform, sucking in deeply the cool night air as we ran. By this hour it had turned quite chilly, in pleasant contrast to the heat we had experienced during the afternoon. We sprinted all the way to the end of the platform, laughing and giggling like children. Tamara was running forward and I was running backward, barely managing to stay ahead of her. When we reached the end of the platform we stopped for a moment to catch our breath, then leisurely began walking back toward our coach.

"Do you have fun like this in America?" Tamara asked me.

"Not exactly like this," I replied.

"What kind of fun do you have, then?" she asked.

I couldn't very well explain what the difference was, except to point out that in America you wouldn't so often find a schoolteacher, a foreigner, a surgeon, and a train conductor running wildly down a railway platform together at midnight.

Felix lit up a cigarette, then handed it over to me. I took a few puffs and passed it on to Dr. Viktor, who after a few drags passed it back to Felix. We barely had time to finish smoking it before the train began moving again and we had to leap back aboard.

Lying in my bunk that night I could only look back on this day as one of the most remarkable of my life. Although the things we did and said were simple enough, they were the sort of things I knew even then would glitter in my memory forever. I turned over once—to gaze at the stars glinting across the boundless Siberian night—and then I fell asleep.

JULY 15—*I feel as though I have been on the fast train* Russia *half my life. There is something about being aboard a moving train, covering immense distances, that seems to defy, almost to defeat, time itself—because there is perpetual movement and activity; something is always happening, even when nothing is. The scenes, the situations, the people are constantly changing. Nothing is static. One minute I am playing chess or* durak *or dominoes, the next minute gazing out the window at the shifting landscape, trying to communicate with someone in sign language . . . then hopping off the train, running through a new village or station, leaping back aboard, peering at still another landscape, at the same time listening to the soccer games, to the moan of rolling wheels, to the unremitting music with its sometimes haunting melodies. . . . In one sense it is very real and immediate; and on another level, almost dreamlike. . . .*

Vaguely, I remember Vova shaking me in the very early hours of the morning to look out at the shadowy Irtysch River just after we stopped at a city called Omsk, but nobody else on the coach was stirring and we soon went back to sleep. Hours later, though it seemed like a moment, Tamara tapped me on the shoulder and said, "Wake up. It's a beautiful day and time for breakfast."

I rolled over slowly, squinting at Tamara's luminous smile. The sunlight was pouring through the window, bathing her face in a radiant glow. "What time is it?" I asked.

"It's time to eat," she said, laughing.

At breakfast, Tamara taught me a few more Russian words, and when I got back to the compartment I wrote them down in the back of my journal. I counted up the total and found that I now had a Russian vocabulary of nearly a hundred words, most of which I pronounced very well, Tamara said.

Later that morning Dr. Viktor came by and trounced me in a game of dominoes, but I beat him in tic-tac-toe. I had just finished playing another song on my fist for Yuri and Lenya when the train made a short stop at Tyumen, an ancient-looking city of over 250,000, which Tamara informed me was Siberia's oldest settlement. When we stopped I grabbed my camera from my suitcase. I had taken very few pictures thus far on the trip, but this seemed like a good place to get some. We hurried down the platform to the food stalls. On the way back I lined up the passengers who were walking with me and took a number of quick shots. Then I handed the camera to Dr. Viktor and he snapped a picture of Tamara and me, surrounded by Lyuda and Mikhail and Felix and a number of the children. Mikhail put his conductor's hat on my head and I crouched down and did an awkward rendition of a cossack dance, which prompted a rousing chorus of laughter and applause.

After lunch, we listened to the soccer games and then everybody crowded into our compartment to hear Indira Gandhi's speech on Radio Moscow. Mrs. Gandhi had come to Russia to promote peace talks, but from what she said it appeared the talks had scant hopes of succeeding, which for a while left us a little less cheerful.

Later that afternoon we left the high plateau we'd been crossing all morning, descending to a lower but still woodsy country, and stopped finally at another large industrial city called Sverdlovsk, where Czar Nicholas and his family were executed in 1918, and near where Francis Gary Powers was forced down in his reconnaissance plane in 1960. At Sverdlovsk Tamara and Felix and I made a mad sprint into town. Looking back, it seems incredible how we were able to take advantage of every single second on stops such as these. We hit the pavement running and were literally halfway into the city before the train came to a complete halt. We grabbed some cups of ice cream—on the run, practically—then dashed between a taxi and two buses, then straight down what looked like a main street and on through a department store where Tamara and Felix made some hasty purchases; then we hurried on back toward the station.

When we came in sight of the platform we could see the train already beginning to move out. "Oh, God," I thought, "after all our close shaves this is where we get left." But we shifted our course sharply, Tamara yelling, "Come on, come on!" and took a short cut between two large warehouses—then, with a final burst of speed, we leaped back aboard at the last possible moment.

Until we were safely back on the train we had little time to consider the consequences of being left behind, but just inside the exit, bent over double and gasping for breath, we suddenly began to think about it. And the more we thought about it, the funnier it became, until finally we were bent over again, this time purely from laughing.

Back inside the compartment I asked Tamara and Felix what they had purchased at the department store—what was so important that had almost caused us to miss our train. They seemed a little evasive, and I was about to question them further when Olya and Nadya walked in. Olya asked me to make her a paper hat like the ones we had seen at various stations along the way. After some difficulty in locating suitable materials (Tamara was nearly an hour in finding a stack of old newspapers in Mikhail's quarters) I set about the task of making a paper hat for Olya, but none of my efforts were very successful. Remembering, however, the way I had made them as a child, I finally got one to turn out right. Tamara wrote Olya's name on one side of the hat and I signed my name on the other. Then I placed the finished product on Olya's head and she beamed proudly.

Naturally, when the other children saw Olya's hat they all wanted their own, so the rest of the afternoon was spent largely in constructing and autographing paper hats. When I had finished a hat for each of the children, I made one for Tamara and she made one for me. We wrote each other's names on one side of each hat and autographed the other side. On my hat Tamara wrote, "Jay, the American," and signed herself "Schoolteacher," and I wrote on hers, "Tamara, who bites people," and signed myself *"Durak."*

Sometime later I recalled that I had made only ten hats, and there were eleven children on our coach. Then I remembered that Marina had not been present with the rest of the children. I walked down the corridor about halfway to the far exit until I found her compartment. When Marina saw me walk in, she turned her head away, toward the window. She was sitting by the table, next to another child who was wearing one of the hats I had made. I tried to explain to Marina (and to her parents) that she had not been forgotten, that I was in the process of making a hat for her, too. Her parents smiled when they understood what I was trying to say, and I was hoping Marina would turn back around and speak, but she just kept staring out the window.

Returning to our compartment, I finished Marina's hat. It was an especially fine one, I thought, made of bright blue and yellow wrapping paper that Tamara brought back from the "hard-class" section. On the top of the hat I taped a small fragment of pink ribbon and on one side of it I wrote, "Marina, a very pretty young lady," and on the other side, "Jay, your friend." Then I went back to her compartment and placed the hat very gently on her head. Delighted, her parents tried to get Marina to show some sign of appreciation, but she only looked away uneasily, as though she wanted to smile but couldn't, and snuggled up closer to her mother. Her parents seemed embarrassed at her behavior, but there wasn't much to say about it, so I smiled and returned to our compartment, disappointed that apparently nothing I could do would break the barrier between us.

Later that afternoon, not long after leaving Sverdlovsk, a number of the passengers began crowding the windows, pointing. We were winding slowly through the comparatively low but rocky Ural Mountains. I looked out and saw a bulky, sand-colored obelisk, which Tamara said was the boundary line separating Europe from Asia. We were now at the edge of another continent, having traversed the largest on earth. Most of the rest of the way would be spent going gently downhill, through coniferous forests and wide, unobstructed fields.

Toward dusk the sun appeared locked in position just above the florid horizon. Siberia was finally behind us. It struck me how strange were my feelings. Seven days before, my only concern was how to get through this remote, seemingly forlorn country, how to pass the time.

Now, looking back, I felt a sudden longing for that wild and beautiful land, for the rugged landscape, even for those clusters of intruding industry whose might I had briefly glimpsed—the dusty stretches of workhouses and refineries and truck convoys. It all seemed so familiar now, and I had a fleeting wish that this journey would never end.

I was in the washroom when I felt a faint shift of power in the locomotive and knew instinctively we were approaching another stop. I stepped out of the washroom, noticing that the door to our compartment was closed, then walked quickly down the corridor to Felix's quarters to see if he wanted to leave the train. He did, but he said this would only be a very short stop: we would have to hurry if we wanted to make it to the stalls and back. So without delay Felix and I walked back down to my compartment to get Tamara and to get ready for another quick run to some of the kiosks along the platform, just as we had done so many times (it seemed like hundreds of times) before. But when we slid back the door to the compartment Tamara was standing there, in her best clothes, with a small bag in one hand and a large suitcase in the other. I had never seen her dressed up before. There was powder on her cheeks and a dash of dark red on her lips, and tilted back slightly on her head was the paper hat I'd made her a few hours before. The hat gave her the appearance of a well-dressed clown, and for a moment I felt like laughing—until I realized what the occasion was. I knew Tamara was scheduled to leave the train sometime before we got to Moscow, but I hadn't thought that it would be so soon. In the midst of all the furious activity of the past few days, I'd lost track of time, but now the certainty of her leaving impaled me like a knife. My heart sank, numbing me into silence.

It happened so quickly then: the *Russia* came crunching to a halt. Tamara smiled and extended her hand. I lamely offered her mine, hardly saying a word. Politely, she said that she had enjoyed knowing me, that she wished me the best of luck in my life. Then she smiled once more, picked up her bags, and walked on down the corridor to the exit.

Later, when I tried to reconstruct the scene, I thought there must have been more to it than that. There should have been more regrets, a little more anguish or pain . . . perhaps even a few tears. Two people could not have lived so closely, crossing an entire continent together, and have that relationship end so abruptly. It should have been only the beginning of a lifelong friendship—not the end. But that was all I could remember. Tamara stepped down onto the platform and stood there on the pavement, waving to the passengers on our coach who were crowding the windows and waving back. Suddenly the train began moving again—and she was gone.

I have been lying here on my bunk for the last two hours, staring vacantly at the ceiling. It is time for supper, I know, and I

*should be going to the diner, but I don't feel
like eating. I don't feel like doing anything
except dropping off to sleep, but I can't manage that because I'm not even drowsy. All I
can think about is Tamara's absence and the
fact that she is back there—back in some
nameless village on the edge of Siberia some
fifty or sixty miles away by now, and out of
our lives forever. . . .*

It was nearly three hours after Tamara left the train that
I finally got up from my bunk and went to the diner. It
was dark now and I still wasn't hungry, but I decided I'd
better get some food in my stomach or I'd never get to
sleep. When I reached the diner Felix and Vova and
Natasha and Yuri were sitting there, staring out the window. They seemed glad to see me, but none of them said
very much while I was eating. Once I remarked that there
were no flowers on any of the tables this evening, and
when Felix told Vova and Natasha what I had said, I saw
them exchange quick, knowing glances. But the absence
of flowers seemed appropriate to the occasion. We had sat
here so many times before, the six of us, chatting merrily,
with Tamara laughing and explaining our comments to
one another. We were like one big family; but now we
seemed more like distant cousins, unable to express our-
selves to each other, reduced once again to basic signs and
gestures. The little German I knew was enough to con-

vey only the simplest thoughts: "Tamara is gone and so are the flowers."

"Ja, Tamara ist gegangen so wie die Blumen."

We sat in the dining car until closing time, only occasionally speaking. Sometimes the silence grew embarrassing. We went back to the compartment and played a quiet game of *durak*. Then Felix left and we all went to bed.

JULY 16—11:35 A.M. *Nearing lunchtime.*
The morning broke amid verdant grain
fields and glistening forests as the fast train
Russia *bears swiftly toward Moscow, as if*
impatient to end its spun-out journey. The
birch trees are still with us, I see, but the
leaves seem greener now and the bark whiter.
Above the fields and the forests the early
morning sun is flaring from a cloudless sky
and the music, now sad and doleful, is bro-
ken only occasionally by a long, lingering
whistle from the straining locomotive. . . .

Breakfast was much like supper the night before, except that Felix was not at the table. His place was occupied by Dr. Viktor, who could not even speak German, so there was barely any communication at all. We played tic-tac-toe on a napkin for a while and spent the rest of the time staring wistfully out the window.

Later that morning we crossed the fabled Volga River, with its winsome waters and tree-lined banks, and from the bridge we caught a clear view of the city of Yaroslavl, with its stark white walls and gleaming church domes. Just beyond the belfry of its *kremlin,* we could see Tugovaya Hill, where the townspeople once mourned the dead who had fallen in battle against the Tatars.

Perhaps an hour later we reached Aleksandrov, which Felix said was the last major stop before reaching Moscow. At Aleksandrov he and Dr. Viktor and I jumped off the train, but this debarking was without any rush or excitement. The passengers were calm and restrained, and nobody seemed to be going anywhere: everyone was just stretching their legs and walking leisurely about. Something else was different, too—none of the passengers were in their pajamas or casual clothes; they were all dressed up in their best suits and skirts. They almost seemed like strangers again, as when they first boarded at Khabarovsk. The children especially looked different.

Strangest of all was the fact that after only three minutes or so the passengers began boarding again, well before the train started rolling. Felix and Dr. Viktor, standing on opposite sides of me, began nudging me toward the coach door.

"What's the big hurry?" I asked. "The train's not even moving yet."

All Felix would say was that it was time to get back on.

I should have expected something unusual was in the making, but I didn't. When we stepped back onto the train I saw that the entire end of our coach was packed with people, most of whom I knew, but there were also passengers from the other coaches. Felix and Dr. Viktor pushed me on through the crowd, the three of us finally squeezing into my compartment, where Vova and Natasha were standing near the window waiting to shake my hand. Mikhail and Ilya and Yuri and some of the children were sitting on the top bunks, dangling their legs. Only when Felix said, *"Ein Fest für Sie,"* did I realize what was happening.

"A party for me?" I said.

Then the gifts began pouring forth: Lyuda presented me with a book, with a sketch of herself on the inside flap and an inscription which was signed by all the passengers on our coach. Several other people handed me gifts, among which were a stickpin, some wooden dolls, several packs of cigarettes, and a pair of gold cuff links. Then Dr. Viktor handed me a present, which he indicated was from Felix and someone not present. It was the only gift that was wrapped. I untied the ribbon, regretting I had nothing to give anyone, and ashamed that the idea had not even occurred to me until now. I peeled the wrapping off and found in a small brown box a miniature bronze *Sputnik*, with a note attached. It read: "Jay—we will never forget you and we hope you will not forget us." The note was not signed, but when Felix announced to the passengers that the present was from Tamara (which spurred everyone to cheer) I realized why we had run so frantically through the streets of Sverdlovsk and why we had come so harrowingly close to missing the train.

Before I could recover from this, Mikhail opened a large bottle of champagne, and when everyone in the compartment had a small glass, he offered a toast, followed by many from the others. The only part I understood, of course, was the warm spirit in which they were offered. When it came my turn, I sputtered a few words in English, which drew warm, uncomprehending smiles. Then, remembering one of the words Tamara taught me, I held my glass up high and said in a loud voice, "*Mir,*" which means peace, and their faces brightened into broad grins, after which they broke into shouts and clapped uproariously, resounding, "*Mir! Mir! Mir!*"

As the train began pulling out, a number of the children from our coach were ushered to the doorway, where Lenya and Nadya presented me with a fountain pen. And then, still wearing the paper hats I had made them the day before, they broke into a song—a beautiful, haunting melody that Tamara had taught them. The song lingered in my ears long after the gathering had disassembled and the passengers vanished to their separate retreats, long after the engine had resumed its speed and the rumble and roar of the wheels once again engulfed the corridor. . . .

The last hour of the journey to Moscow was quiet and uneventful. I sat by the window, watching the soft, silent fields slowly disappear, to be replaced gradually by smoking chimneys, factories, and huddles of brown and yellow apartment houses—until finally the great city of Moscow rose sharply into view.

A little after noon we pulled slowly into Yaroslavsky Station, a facsimile of a Russian fairy castle. When we came to a stop, the passengers quickly dispersed and went their various ways amid the bustle and clatter of the terminal. I stood there a moment after climbing off the fast train *Russia* and watched them disappear one by one— until all of them had vanished and I was alone. Then I turned and walked quickly away, toward the waiting room.

EPILOGUE

After I left the train station, I remained in Moscow for the better part of a week, residing at the Hotel Peking just off Gorky Street, not too distant from Red Square. During those five or six days most of my time was spent doing the things tourists usually do: there were visits to the Kremlin, to Lenin's tomb, to the State University, to the G.U.M. department store, a night at the Bolshoi, and so forth—all very interesting and entertaining.

Following my stay in Moscow, I went down to Odessa and spent a few days sunning on the beaches of the Black Sea, after which I traveled on to the Holy Land, through Damascus and Jerusalem, then back to Beirut. From there I went to Cairo and Luxor, and finally to Piraeus, from which port I sailed back to America in early September.

There were many compelling and exciting things that happened to me after I left the Soviet Union. In Egypt I swam in the Nile River and in Greece I climbed Mount Olympus. And all through the Middle East, through those turbulent, sun-drenched lands, poignant situations seemed to confront me at every turn. But whatever else I experienced during that summer of my around-the-world voyage, the episode that shines most fervidly in my memory is that wonderful journey across the plains of Siberia. . . .

It has been nearly two decades now since I said goodbye to my friends at Yaroslavsky Station, but over the years I have thought of them often—in the fall of the year mostly, it seems—especially at those times when I am lonely or weary or disheartened, as I was when I first came to know them. And occasionally I pause to wonder what has become of them. Do they remember me as I remember them? Is Tamara still the bright shimmering light I once knew? She must be in her mid-forties by now, entering middle age, as I am also. And what has become of Nadya and Olya —those dazzling little pixies with the twinkling eyes? They would be all grown now, of course, perhaps married, perhaps with children of their own . . .

And what of little Yuri? I suppose he's a merchant seaman, like his father. And the old cossack? And Lyuda and Mikhail and Dr. Viktor?

Not infrequently, as I recall those faded images of the past, I begin to hear their voices. I begin to see their shadowed faces moving with me across the enchanted fields and forests . . . and once again I hear the merry laughter of children mingled with the roll of steel, with the timeless music and the whir and roar of the fast train *Russia*. . . .

There is one incident in particular that keeps coming back to me, like a recurring dream. That last night in the dining car, a few hours after Tamara left the train, we were sitting at the table—Felix and Vova and Natasha and I—the same evening I happened to remark that there were no more flowers on the tables. There was a perfectly logical reason for this, as I later found out, but at the time I was unaware of it. I noticed, however, the quick, curious glances exchanged between Felix and Natasha. I thought nothing of it then, but evidently they must have decided that flowers had an unusually special meaning for me (though I'm sure I have no greater or lesser concern for them than the next person) and word spread quickly among the passengers of our coach that the American was distressed by the absence of flowers. As I later learned just before we arrived in Moscow—it was Vova who told me, through Felix's moving gestures—when we made a stop very early on that last morning, just barely after the sun had risen, a determined little girl, whose name neither Vova nor Felix could recall, left the train (the only person to get off at that station) and made her way across the tracks to the nearby woods and back. When I arrived at breakfast later that morning for our last meal, there—on my table only—was a small jar brimming with bright, freshly picked wild flowers. Even now I can see Felix trying to convey to me the awkward movements of the little girl who fetched them; even now I can see him pantomiming that young child's limping gait. . . .